5-28-24

calibrates as truth as true

Discovery of the
Presence of God

Devotional Nonduality

Also by David R. Hawkins

Transcending the Levels of Consciousness:
The Stairway to Enlightenment

Truth vs. Falsehood: How to Tell the Difference

I: Reality and Subjectivity

The Eye of the I: From Which Nothing Is Hidden

Power vs. Force: The Hidden Determinants
of Human Behavior

Dialogues on Consciousness and Spirituality

Qualitative and Quantitative Analysis and Calibration of the
Levels of Human Consciousness

Orthomolecular Psychiatry (with Linus Pauling)

Discovery of the
Presence of God

Devotional Nonduality

David R. Hawkins, M.D., Ph.D.

VERITAS

Veritas Publishing
P. O. Box 3516
W. Sedona, AZ 86340
Phone: 928-282-8722 • Fax: 928-282-4789
www.veritaspub.com

Hardbound ISBN: 0-9715007-7-0
Softbound ISBN: 0-9715007-6-2

Straight and narrow is the path . . .
Waste no time.
Gloria in Excelsis Deo!

TABLE OF CONTENTS

FOREWORD

Prior written works plus recorded lectures have provided an organized body of information and verifiable data that have occasioned numerous study groups worldwide and translation of the works into the world's major languages. Consciousness research has resulted in the widespread dissemination of essential information not previously available to mankind.

While the primary thrust of consciousness research was to facilitate spiritual awareness and identify verifiable truth, it was also educative to apply the same techniques to elucidate the evolution of consciousness and its expressions over time as various facets of civilization and history, as reported in Truth vs. Falsehood. These included a study of the world's great religions and the verification of teachers and teachings of spiritual truth over the ages, which are of great pragmatic value to the spiritual seeker.

The totality of the foregoing results in a distillation of critical premises that constitute the essentials which need to be known in order to facilitate the evolution of spiritual consciousness in the individual seeker. This is especially so for the serious devotee of spiritual truth as the pathway to Enlightenment. The way is both confirmable and subjectively experiential. Thus, the pathway of Devotional Nonduality is a direct course to Enlightenment via clarification of core essentials that merely await activation by decision, intention, and dedication of the will.

While revered literature and scripture by teachers of spiritual truth and enlightenment are available worldwide, their historic works were not written, verbalized, or contextualized for ready comprehension by the modern person who is now more formally educated. The current human mind is often put off by seemingly extraneous teachings that are intertwined with traditional religions, such as unfamiliar languaging or ecclesiastical doctrine that incorporates primarily ethnic observances of time and location. By over-inclusion, the extraneous becomes confused with the essential, thereby decreasing appeal as well as credibility and clarity.

For truth to be true, it must be so throughout time, which means, therefore, that it must be verifiable and confirmable in the present day as well. The Realization of Truth is thus not only a radical, experiential, subjective state but also a condition that is confirmable by the methodology of consciousness research. Thus, the Reality of a spiritual state is verifiable both from 'within' (experiential subjectivity) and from 'without' (confirmable objectivity), i.e., validated by Descartes' *res interna* (cogitans) as well as *res extensa* (the world as it is). Therefore, in order to serve the objective requirements, included are the calibrated levels of all chapters, the work as a whole, and important statements. In addition, in Appendix C there is a description of the simple technique whereby any integrous person can independently confirm the level of truth of any statement or principle, the validity of which does not depend on a specific teaching or belief system.

PREFACE

The discovery of the method of how to tell truth from falsehood, and also how to calibrate the verifiable degree of levels of truth, opened up for examination and redefinition the entire human experience over vast periods of time in all of its cultures and expressions. As in the discovery of the compass, telescope, or computer, the new information recontextualizes common human beliefs and experiences and examines them from a higher perspective and clarity of definition.

Like prior advances of knowledge, new discoveries result in a mixed response of excitement and pleasure from the more adventurous to argument and resistance from the pessimist or skeptic. Thus, while part of the mind is stimulated and uplifted by new discovery, another part longs to cling to the familiar, even if it is flawed or grossly incorrect.

New discovery brings challenge as well as promise, and actual value is derived from practice, application, and experience over time. Of value in the advances in the understanding of consciousness are redefinition, clarification, and recontextualization that reveal new meanings and comprehension at greater depth.

What follows is a distillation of pragmatic applications of confirmable truth for seriously committed spiritual endeavor, and to that end is this work dedicated.

*Gloria
in
Excelsis Deo!*

INTRODUCTION

The straightest way to spiritual evolution and advanced states of consciousness is via the field of consciousness itself, which is the nonlinear Radiance of Divine Energy that is the substrate of all that exists. The condition of Enlightenment is the state of pure Radiance that shines forth as the Presence/Self. The Self is the essence of spiritual existence and Reality as subjectively Known by virtue of effulgent Identity.

The Radiance and Effulgence of the nonlinear Self are autonomous, consequent to relinquishment of the linear/ego positionalities and emotions that preclude their realization. The phenomenon of Enlightenment is thus analogous to the shining forth of the sun when the clouds have been removed. The radiance of the sun cannot be 'acquired', 'forced', or 'obtained', all of which are linear concepts consequent to the suppositions of the ego/mind's belief in cause and effect.

There is no 'cause' in Enlightenment anymore than there is a 'cause' of God. Such ideas represent misconceptions of theology and limitations of the dualistic, linear ego/mind. Thus, one does not 'get' Enlightenment, nor is there any personal self to whom the condition could be applied, much less held as a quality or attribute.

The way to Enlightenment is simply that of surrendering the barriers that preclude the state of Realization. The personal self, therefore, does not become enlightened but instead falls away and is replaced by the previously obscured Reality of the Self as the Radiance of God Immanent. This is in contrast to linear concepts and beliefs about God as being primarily only transcendent and therefore 'elsewhere' in time and location.

The purpose of the work here presented is to share the subjective unfoldment of Inner Realization in such a manner that it potentiates the process in the student and provides the essential information that facilitates the major evolution of the Subjectivity of Reality to Awareness. The intention is to potentiate the spiritual aspirant's inner search for the ultimate source of Existence as the Radiant Divinity that is simultaneously 'within' and 'without', and simultaneously neither, yet both.

The pathway described represents the concordance of Devotion and Truth plus intention and inspirational confirmation by experiential and testimonial declaration. Thus, the literary style is declarative rather than the customary provisional or tentative. The Inner Reality resonates as the Absolute, which is of a different quality as a consequence of its Source. The style of presentation is itself designed to facilitate the resonance of recognition that awaits activation in the seeker since the Self of the reader and the writer are actually one and the same.

To summarize, the purpose of this presentation is to provide the essential information needed to successfully pursue the pathway to Enlightenment, along with practical guidelines and methods of applying the information to the seeker's personal inner states of spiritual evolution. Therefore, what follows is neither philosophy nor metaphysics, neither pedagogy nor theology, but is instead a distillation of the core truths of Spiritual Reality as they become progressively discernable and experientially comprehensible along the progressive path.

Because spiritual evolution does not proceed along a logical, linear, definable, predictable timeline, what could be considered very advanced instruction is presented from the very beginning and recurrently throughout this treatise/manual. Important themes are represented, as comprehension is facilitated by context and familiarity.

Herein is provided all that one needs to know to reach the state or condition of consciousness termed Enlightened/Self-Realization/Jivanmukta/Liberation (calibrates as true).

The Spiritual Process

Section One

Overview

The ultimate Truth is radically subjective and also confirmable by consciousness research. Both ways will be described in the sequence of their emergence with the development of an empirical science of consciousness. Subjective, experiential mystical states of advanced awareness and enlightenment can now be verified objectively by a method that transcends both time and place.

Subjective: Experiential

Prior to age three, there was oblivion. Then, out of the void of nothingness, there arose a sudden and shocking awareness of personal existence, as though a strong light had been turned on. Spontaneously, unwelcome and without words, came the awareness of existence itself as the experiential basis of the subjective state. Almost immediately arose the fear of its seeming opposite—the hypothetical possibility of nonexistence. Thus, at age three, there was confrontation with the dualities of existence versus nonexistence as the Ultimate Reality, and the polarity of the Ultimate Reality as Allness versus nothingness. The experience was totally nonverbal but overwhelmingly and starkly confrontive.

Ordinary childhood activities were boring, and refuge was sought in philosophy and an introspective, introverted lifestyle. Academic success was easy and led to the eager reading of Plato, Aristotle, Plotinus, and others whose minds had become mental companions. On the other hand, beauty was entrancing, and appreciation for the great cathedrals and sacred classical music led to the study of music and voice as a boy soprano in the choir of a great cathedral.

Home life was rural and Episcopal. Late one day, as a paperboy in a blizzard after dark, refuge was sought from 10-below-zero winds. Relief was found in a hollowed-out snow bank, and then emerged the exquisite onset of a state of consciousness in which the mind melted and became silent. A Presence—timeless, gentle, yet infinitely powerful—pervaded, and its overwhelming Love replaced mentalization.

Time stopped and the awareness of Oneness with eternity replaced all thought or sense of a personal self. The 'I-ness' of the Presence revealed itself as Allness. It was knowable as being beyond all universes—unspeakable, invisible, all pervading, inexplicable, and beyond names. Subsequently, all fear of death disappeared, and life continued spontaneously of its own accord. This state was never mentioned to anyone.

Then came World War II and hazardous duty on a minesweeper, which was facilitated by the loss of the fear of death. The demands of earthly life insisted on being given attention and involvement. The reenergizing of the intellect enabled successful academic years, graduation from medical school, plus years spent in psychiatry and psychoanalysis. The development of a huge psychiatric practice in New York followed. After twenty-five years of exhausting work, the yearning to return to the Truth and the Presence of God as the State of Bliss led to a resumption of intensive meditation.

One day, while walking in the woods, there came unasked a massive revelation of the totality of human suffering throughout all time which resulted in an overwhelming feeling of shock and dismay that 'God could allow such conditions to occur'. The mind blamed God and then became atheistic. The burning question still persisted: If there was no God, then what was the core of the truth of existence?

Buddhism was attractive because it avoided the use of the term 'God'. There was despair at having lost the revelation of Reality. This led to intense meditation and a driven inner searching for Truth itself, eventually resulting in severe existential depression and desperation.

As the depths of the psyche were explored with fixity of purpose, the intense meditative state led to realms of severe despair and eventually to the depths of hell in timeless dimensions of eternal agony in which one is forever cut off from the Light. The depths are endless, and one comes to the knowingness of the meaning of "abandon hope all ye who enter here." The terror of eternal isolation followed without any hope of its termination or even relief by extermination, for there was not even the possibility of death as the ultimate escape.

Next followed the surrender of hope itself, which was replaced by a timeless dread. Then, from within, a silent voice cried out, "If there is a God, I ask for help." This was followed by oblivion, and then the mind went into a state of silence.

Finally, awareness returned, but the appearance of the world had changed and was dramatically transformed. It was now a silent, unified Oneness, magnifi-

cent in its brilliance that shone forth the Divinity of all
existence. It magnified a single remaining discordant
disparity—the persistence of a personal sense of a self
as the core of one's life and existence. It was clear that
this also had to be surrendered to the Presence. Then
the fear of real death arose as terror. But with the terror also came the knowingness of an instruction from
Zen Buddhism: "Walk straight ahead, no matter what—
all fear is illusion."

The necessity to abandon and surrender the identity
of self as the source of one's existence was a powerful
knowingness. The will to live, the seeming core of life
itself, was then surrendered to God, followed by a few
moments of terrifying agony and then the experience
of death itself. This was unlike bodily death where one
finds oneself suddenly free and looking at the body
lying there, which had happened several times previously. No, this is the first and only time that death
can be experienced. The finality of the death was
overwhelming. At last, the agony was over and was
replaced by splendor and magnificence—infinite stillness, silence, and the peace of profound Infinite Love.
The mind was dumbfounded and overwhelmed with
awe. It then became silent and disappeared.

Henceforth, only the Presence prevailed and all
emerged autonomously without a personal will or
motivation. The condition was a permanent replacement of the personal self—a silent, universal, timeless
Presence by which the totality of Allness replaces any
prior states of consciousness or the presumption of a
personal self or 'I'.

Curiously, without motivation, the body moved
spontaneously and continued to perform activities that

were autonomous as there was no 'thinker' to think, no 'planner' to plan, nor any 'doer' to do. All occurred of its own essence as potentiality expressed itself as actuality. The condition can best be described as the Unmanifest's becoming Manifest. Henceforth, life unfolded on its own. The condition was unspeakable, and no mention of it was made to anyone for more than thirty years. The condition eventually required leaving ordinary worldly life and moving to a remote rural area for years of meditation, solitude, and adjustment to the state.

Within the condition, understandings spontaneously arose that were without thought. As a prior Hinayana Buddhist, I had believed that the ultimate reality of the Buddha nature was 'Nothingness', or 'Void'. That was an error because voidness itself is a belief system that, however, had recurred as an experiential reality during meditations in this lifetime.

With the constant pursuit of the pathway of negation (attachment or aversion to form), the condition of voidness would return—enormously impressive, infinite, beyond space, time, or description; omnipresent, all-pervasive, and beyond all thought or volition. Yet, despite its seeming nonlinear totality, there was the awareness of the absence of a critical quality that had been experienced as a youth in the snow bank—the exquisite softness, the at-homeness, the familiarity, the recognition of the essence of the totality of Reality as all-inclusive Love. This quality of Love is beyond joy or ecstasy and is intrinsic to the state of Peace.

Strikingly, the Void is very similar to the Ultimate State, except that it is devoid of the Love that is the very essence of Divinity. Without Love, the Void is like infinite, timeless, empty space. Devoid of the quality that identifies it as Divinity, the Void is a limitation. This appeared to be the final, great polarity/duality of the seeming opposites, the resolution of which permitted the Realization of the Self as the Allness and Oneness out of which Creation emerges. (The above paragraph calibrates at 1,000.)

The Development of Consciousness Research

After years of solitude, there was a stirring to once again include the world. People asked questions, and so a sharing/teaching function began. Yet, there was still no way to explain the inner state or demonstrate a pathway other than by the traditional modes of providing information, inspiration, and instruction on meditation.

Then, fortuitously, there was an invitation to attend a lecture on kinesiology in a class taught by Dr. John Diamond. While the class and the teacher contextualized the kinesiological response as a local phenomenon, it was witnessed by this state of consciousness as an impersonal response of universal consciousness itself. It was obvious that the field of consciousness is like an infinite, motionless electrostatic field capable of responding concordantly to the level of strength of the energy of a stimulus.

It was easily demonstrated that what is true or pro-life resulted in a positive response ("yes"). In contrast to falsehood or a stimulus of energy inimical to life, the response was muscular weakness (a "no"). Then it became clear that the response was actually not a "yes" versus a "no," but a "yes" or a "not yes."

With study, the kinesiological response was found

to occur along a gradient that was aligned with the level of energy of a stimulus. A spectrum of responses appeared concordant with the quality of the stimulus. This observation led to the experimental improvisation of an arbitrary mathematical scale.

Critical to the development of an empirical clinical science of consciousness calibration research was a fortuitous observation that whereas fluorescent light, pesticides, and artificial sweeteners made everyone go weak, they did not do so in a group of students of A Course in Miracles after they had progressed to about Lesson 75 (the Course consists of 365 daily lessons). Thus, the kinesiological response was related to the level of consciousness (cessation of seeing oneself as a victim of external 'causes' and re-owning one's power).

By research and observation, it was discovered that all life in all its expressions reflects an innate level of energy, from weak to strong. This spectrum led itself to the development of a calibratable numerical scale that proved, however, to be impractical due to the extreme numbers that were required to keep pace with their numerical designation. This problem was solved by utilizing a logarithmic scale (to the base 10) that permitted the pragmatic use of an arbitrary scale ranging from 1 to 1,000.

Calibration level '1' reflected the first discernible energy of life (consciousness) on this planet (bacteria) and continued through the plant and animal kingdoms to level 1,000 as the ultimate possibility on earth. Level 1,000 turned out to be the consciousness level reached by only a few people in all of human history—the great avatars, such as Jesus Christ, the Buddha, Krishna, and Zoroaster.

The energy-spectrum scale numerically reflected the calibration of the consciousness level of all possibilities of animal or human life. By use of the scale, one could track the evolution of consciousness from its first appearance as life to its ultimate expression as the state of Enlightenment itself.

There followed years of research and application of calibrating the consciousness levels of thousands of individuals, places, concepts, writings, belief systems, emotions, intellectual levels, and even more importantly, all spiritual states, religions, spiritual teachers, spiritual pathways, saints, and sages. In every religion, the mystics (i.e., Self-realized, Enlightened) calibrated the highest on the scale of consciousness but were very few in number.

On the calibrated scale, 600 was the level that differentiated enlightened states of nonduality from saintly, unconditional states that calibrate in the high 500s and include many spiritual teachers and famous saints. Level 500 indicated a change in paradigm from intellectualization to experiential subjectivity and denoted various levels of love. It was also notable that only 4.0 percent of the world's population reached calibration level 500, and only 0.4 percent reached level 540 (Unconditional Love). Consciousness level 600 was extremely rare.

The level of the 400s represents intellect, reason, logic, science, and the Newtonian paradigm. For most educated spiritual seekers, the 400s represent a springboard but also often a great barrier, and it is notable that Einstein, Freud, and Sir Isaac Newton all calibrated at 499. The 200s and 300s indicate integrity, goodwill, morality, and overall goodness of intention.

Then came the crucial discovery that consciousness level 200 is critical because it demarcates truth from falsehood. It was also noted that levels above 200 represent power, and those below 200 represent force. The levels below 200 descend into the obvious egotisms as well as animal instincts of pride, desire, greed, anger, hate, guilt, shame, and apathy. The calibrated levels also correlate with the capacity for spiritual insight, emotionality, and perceptions of the world and self. The calibrated scale and its correlations enabled the construction of the now widely known *Map of Consciousness*.

The ego/mind is a dualistic construction that originated as animal consciousness which, eons later, evolved through primitive hominids and finally to *Homo sapiens*, in which a prefrontal cortex was added to the old animal brain, providing the capacity for linear conceptual thought. Thus, initially, the mind primarily became a new tool for the expression of animal instincts through what is now called the ego.

Examination of the mind structure shows that its function is comparable to the hardware of a computer, and the software represents the programming by society as well as by inherited influences. The fundamental innocence of mankind is based on the reality that the human mind is incapable of discerning truth from falsehood. It has no innate defense against the utilization of its hardware to play any introduced software program without prior approval, discernment, or options of the will (e.g., the impact of the media).

Due to the nature of the software and the underlying hardware, the mind's primary illusion is the differentiation of consciousness into a basic duality of a personal

I/ego/self as being separate from the Infinite Self as the source of consciousness/awareness. In this illusory error, the ego identifies with content instead of context and is therefore subject to the vicissitudes of animal motives, feelings, and faulty intellection.

The calibrated level of consciousness indicates the degree of impairment of the capacity for recognition of Reality by substitution of perception, distortion, and the misidentification of appearance with essence. Also of great interest was the discovery that every single action, feeling, or thought registers permanently beyond time and space in the all-encompassing contextual field of consciousness. Therefore, any event, whether a thought, feeling, or action, is forever identifiable and retrievable by appropriate means, such as the consciousness calibration technique.

The fields of consciousness consist of energy vibrations whose patterns leave a distinguishable track and are experienced as subjectivity. Out of the patterning of the vibrational track arise the forms inherent in karmic consequences of acts of the will. The dualistic structure of the ego stems from the core factor of linear positionality. A centralizing image of a personal self emerges as the belief of an individual personal self as an agent, i.e., the 'thinker' of thoughts, the 'doer' of actions, and the repository of guilt and self-blame. Some qualities are rejected and become buried in the unconscious, along with their emotions, which are the residuals of animal instincts.

Only after evolution to consciousness level 200 does an etheric brain emerge that is functionally capable of spiritual awareness, intention, and karmic responsibility. Naïvely, personal consciousness identifies the self with body, mind, and emotions. Then, by good fortune or as a result of karmic 'merit', spiritual truth is heard and becomes inspirational, and, with further good fortune, a spiritual teacher is encountered. The high vibrational frequencies of the teacher's aura activate the nascent, etheric, higher spiritual bodies in the spiritual student.

The activation of the etheric brain in higher spiritual beings is a consequence of the rising of the *kundalini*, or spiritual energies, which results not only in the formation of higher spiritual bodies and the etheric brain but also actually changes the physiology of the human brain, which now tracks incoming stimuli differently. The person becomes more 'right brain'. Below consciousness level 200, an incoming stimulus is rapidly radiated to the emotional centers, whereas, in a spiritually-oriented person, the faster track goes from stimulus to prefrontal cortex and then to the emotional center. In highly-evolved spiritual people, the incoming information is processed through the etheric prefrontal cortex and then goes by induction to the physical neuronal circuits in the brain.

Below consciousness level 200, animal reactivity predominates as transmission of the incoming information via the prefrontal cortex is slower than the direct route to the emotional center. Thus, below 200, the mind is set for 'fight or flight' or stress responses that disrupt the energy flow through the acupuncture system and are reflected in a negative kinesiological response. Above 200, the processing results in a greater feeling of inner peace and harmony, and the brain neurotransmitters release endorphins rather than adrenalin. (See Brain Physiology Chart, Chapter 6.)

With activation, spiritual energy now flows up the chakra system, out of the base of survival and sexuality, through the spleen of the dark side of emotionality, and up through the solar plexus to activate achievement, aggressive acquisition, and wantingness. With spiritual intentionality and assent of the will, spiritual endeavor then leads to the predominant energy accumulation of the heart at consciousness level 500, reflected as concern for others. Further purification leads to Unconditional Love, which calibrates at 540. The high 500s represent joy and ecstasy, leading to 600, the level of peace and the classic opening of the third eye of discernment of the Buddhic etheric spiritual body.

The consciousness level of mankind evolved very slowly over the millennia. "Lucy," presumably the progenitor of all developmental lines of hominids, emerged approximately three million years ago at calibration level 70. Much later emerged Neanderthal man who calibrated at 75, then Homo erectus at 80, and finally, modern man 600,000 years ago as *Homo sapiens idelta*, at 85. At the time of the birth of the Buddha, the consciousness level of all mankind stood at 90, and by the time of the birth of Jesus Christ, it had reached 100.

The consciousness level of mankind through the last five or six centuries remained at 190, where it stayed until the late 1980s when, coincident with the time of the Harmonic Convergence, it made a spectacular jump to 205. It remained at that level for the next seventeen years, and then suddenly, in November 2003, concomitant with the Harmonic Concordance, it jumped to 207. Interestingly, this significant event was observed and recorded at the end of a lecture given on that day in front of a large audience in San Francisco. At 5:15 PM, the consciousness level was again reaffirmed at its previous level of 205, and by 5:30 PM, it had reached 207, where it remained until recently when it went back down to the present level of 206 due to the impact of the media and world events.

By understanding and accepting the nature of the ego, it is transcended and finally collapses and disappears when all its positionalities and their resultant dualities have been surrendered. The ego does not become enlightened but instead disappears, and a Transcendental Reality replaces it. Just as the sun shines forth when the clouds disappear, the Reality of the Self shines forth of its own as Revelation, Realization, and Enlightenment. Descriptively, it is a condition that replaces the prior state of consciousness. Its occurrence has been subjectively reported as being identical in nature throughout the ages and in all cultures in which all Realized mystics and Avatars agree that it is profound and beyond adequate languaging.

At the last doorway to Enlightenment stands the ego's final challenge, which is the central core belief that it is the source and locus of not only identity but also of life itself. At that point, one is all alone and shorn of all protection or comforting props, belief systems, or even memory. There is solely available within one's aura the high-frequency vibration of the consciousness of the Enlightened Teacher, with its encoded Knowingness. The last step is intuited as a finality from which no turning back is possible, and thus there is consternation at the absoluteness of the finality.

Then arises the knowingness to "walk straight ahead, no matter what, for all fear is illusion." As this last step is taken by the spiritual will, death is experienced, but the fierce anguish lasts for only a few moments. The death of the ego is the only actual death that one can possibly experience, in contrast to which the previous deaths of leaving the body were relatively trivial. The experience of death is terminated by awe at the revelation of the Ultimate Reality, and then even the awe disappears and the Self transcends the duality of Existence versus Nonexistence, Allness versus Nothingness, and Omnipresence versus Void. Even 'is-ness' and 'beingness' are seen as meaningless mentations. The state of Infinite Love dissolves all languaging nouns, adjectives, and verbs, for the Supreme is beyond names or divisions. The Peace of the Silence is the Subjectivity.

Curiously, the body continues to function on its own, without any internal 'doer'. Action occurs of its own without volition or intention. There is the realization that potentiality manifests as the emergence of Evolution as the phenomenon of Creation by which the Unmanifest becomes Manifest. Reality is then realized as context rather than just content.

Life is an expression of eternal consciousness, and therefore, actual, real death is not a possibility, which is a corollary to the more familiar laws of the conservation of energy and matter. Everyone already has a calibratable level of consciousness at birth that is reflective of karmic inheritance. Earthly life can be seen as a staging platform to other dimensional levels of consciousness. Everyone is on an evolutionary journey of that consciousness, and compassion is born out of that realization by the exclamation, *"Gloria in Excelsis Deo!"*

Enlightenment is the consequence of the surrender

of all dualistic illusions to Truth. All suffering ends with dissolution of the ego's positionalities. Thus do we praise the Lord God for radiating Light to the world.

CHAPTER 1

Devotional Nonduality

Introduction

Spiritual evolution is accelerated consequent to intention, alignment, dedication, and clarity, as well as
efficiency of time and effort. Thus, precision of the
process is facilitated by elucidation of its prime
elements and by identification of nonessentials. Many
of these have already been identified in previous
books in these published studies, such as *Truth vs.
Falsehood* (Hawkins, 2005). Thus, aberrant spiritual
teachings can be avoided. Also of benefit are the highly
calibrated teachings and practices that are verifiably
integrous.

Devotion

Spiritual commitment is energized by the alignment of the spiritual will (calibration level 850), with
the attributes of Divinity, which are truth, love, compassion, wisdom, and nonpartiality. Devotion prioritizes
one's life and attracts that which is of assistance. To be
a servant of God is a dedication whereby the goal takes
precedence over all other positionalities, attractions, or
distractions. By devotion and commitment, the pathway unfolds and revelation supplants presumptive
cause-and-effect acquisition. It could be languaged that
the dedication is quite powerfully 'Yang' by intent, but
'Yin' by fulfillment as a process.

All actions become recontextualized, and their spiritual essence begins to shine through appearances.
Devotion also expresses as selfless service whereby
peeling the potatoes is no longer a chore but an act of
love because it has been sanctified by intention.

Eventually all action is dedicated as an act of worship.

Devotion opens up vision, which replaces perception. Only by the surrender that accompanies devotion does intended action reveal itself to be a spontaneous unfolding of the evolution of Creation itself. Devotion to God replaces the ego's devotion to its own self-interest, and one witnesses the effects or consequences of the overall field.

Worship is recontextualized by devotion. It is not done for the benefit of the worshipper or the imaginary benefit to God, but instead, it is merely an acknowledgement of Reality. It is aligned with gratitude for the gift of awareness/consciousness as the Reality of the Knower/Self. It is by virtue of the truth of the Reality of Divinity that the Reality of Divinity can be realized (apperceived and comprehended), which results in gratitude for the capacity for the recognition. Thus, devotion is not the same as piety, nor is it a mood, but instead it is a way of life and a way of being with oneself, God, and the world.

In duality, manifestation is perceived as linear, and therefore, there are both a cause and an effect to be conceptualized and perceived. Positionalities result in perception and vice versa. Thus, the intrinsic spiritual truths of religion (context) became obscured historically by people, places, objects, dates, and ethnic legend (content). Also, by conceptual limitation, Divinity became anthropomorphized and conceived of as having the limitations of human emotional proclivities, such as favoritism, anger, jealousy, pride, and egoistic needs. By analogy, it is apparent that sunlight and the sky merely 'are', without partiality or arbitrary preference.

Despite limitations, within the core of religions is

the primordial spiritual truth from which they arose. Note, however, that religions progressively calibrate lower than the calibrated levels of the truth of their great spiritual teachers, the founders (avatars). Thus, much becomes lost via ecclesiastical doctrine's contamination and dilution by cultural, ethnic, and political splinter subgroups and their belief systems.

Nonduality means to bypass particularization and return to unobstructed, verifiable, basic truth. Throughout history, all the great sages have proclaimed the same truths. Although many great sages began their personal lives with traditional religion, they eventually transcended the institutional limitations. Self-realization resulted in their descriptive categorization or nominalization as 'mystics', about which there is much misinformation due to the lack of accurate understanding of the condition, which is an intrinsic inner state. Transcendence by illumination is statistically unusual and therefore frequently baffles comprehension. Over time, however, mysticism became clarified as the inner pathway to the realization of the religious spiritual truths of God as immanent, rather than, as commonly described religiously, only transcendent. Advanced levels of spiritual evolution, however, were traditionally recognized and often designated as sainthood.

Nonduality means without form, division, or limitation, such as time, locality, or mentalization, including arbitrary linear presumptions. Divinity is, by its innate 'qualities', omniscience, omnipresence, and omnipotence, and all evolves as a consequence of the Unmanifest's becoming Manifest as evolutionary Creation.

Divinity emanates as consciousness/awareness,

which sources Creation in its expression as the emergence of existence. The conditions implied by the terms 'beingness', 'existence', 'awareness', or 'consciousness' are without subject or object and devoid of causal qualities. The Nonlinear is therefore a field of Infinite Power by which manifestation emerges as the consequence of potentiality, which itself is an expression of Creation. Within that which is perceived is the Unseen as the Source of All that Exists.

Devotion to Nonduality

If, in Reality, there is no separate 'this' (me) or elsewhere 'that' (God), how do the illusions of the Unreal become replaced by the Real? The way is not by acquiring even more information or knowledge about God but instead by surrendering all suppositions. The core of devotion is humility and the willingness to surrender all belief systems and illusions of 'I know'.

The Realization of the Presence of Divinity unfolds of its own when the ego and its perceptual positionalities are surrendered. To 'Know', it is necessary to drop the limiting impairment of the illusion of knowing 'about'. The mind collects knowledge, facts, and mentations that are limited by context and paradigm of mentalization. The Realization emerges from a paradigm different from that of the linear, conceptual mind. Thus, mind is replaced by Mind. While mind is talkative, Mind is silent and unmoving, yet do all seeming 'things' move within it. In contrast, evolution appears to ordinary mind as the consequence of cause and effect because of the perceptions of form, time, and change.

Thus, spiritual evolution means to move from identification with content (linear 'mind') to context (nonlinear Mind). Spiritual evolution in itself brings forth the transformation in the nonform of Realization, which is beyond conceptualization or languaging and instead becomes apparent and dominant without the necessity of thought.

Traditionally, the way of Nonduality has been the province of the mystics of all religions who sought the Realization of Truth rather than just worshipping its description. The Buddha thus became perhaps the most well-known and prominent example of the inner journey whereby the illusory world of the ego's Maya is transcended and dissolved by the surrendering of attachments to the sensory linear perceptions that camouflage the Unity and Oneness of Creation. It is the invisible Presence of the Nonlinear within the Linear that gives it reality.

In the Hindu tradition, the Sanskrit term for nonduality is *Advaita* (as exemplified by *Vedanta*), and in the Islamic religion, the nonlinear mode is exemplified by the Sufis. In Christianity, Jesus taught that "heaven is within you," and the great Christian mystics (*Unio Mystica*) were given recognition as saints. Their inner spiritual struggles have been recorded in their autobiographical accounts and have been inspirational and revered over the centuries.

Common to all the above is the core of intense devotion that signifies total commitment to Divinity as both the Means and the End. An unnecessary deterrent to devotees of the inner path in traditional Christianity was the ecclesiastical condemnation of the ego's proclivities as 'sin' rather than as merely developmental delays or obstacles of consciousness itself. As becomes apparent, the ego's original evolutionary purpose was merely to ensure survival in the animal world, which therefore required linear identification of friend from foe, edible from inedible, and so on.

Instinctual drives were religiously labeled as evil and, therefore, because of the nature of the human psyche, they were denied, suppressed, projected onto others, or at least compensated for by guilt, self-condemnation, penance, suffering, or even the payment of money as indulgences or a variety of other (including animal) sacrifices.

These guilty self-condemnations were also a consequence and in accord with primitive views of God as being angry and destructive and therefore having to be appeased. The depictions of really a satanic version of God reached their most grotesque demonstration in the Aztec and Mayan religions, which required the constant sacrifice of endless thousands of humans, especially the innocent young whose hearts were cut out while they were still beating. Such extremes are still actively pursued by fundamentalist factions of religious extremists, such as today's pursuers of theocratic totalitarianism (e.g., ritualistic beheading).

Because of the proclivity of the human ego/mind to embrace very severe error, the Buddha recommended avoiding the use of the term 'God' altogether. In devotional nonduality, the likelihood of error is bypassed by devotion to the essential nonlinear qualities of Divinity itself, such as compassion, oneness, love, truth, omniscience, eternal, infinite, omnipresence, and omnipotence beyond form, place, time, human instincts, or emotions.

Divine Justice rules as a consequence of its intrinsic, innate qualities of infinite power and is not limited by positionalities or volitional qualities. Thus, Divinity is not to be feared but instead highly respected and revered. When the evil depictions of the ego are transcended, it is then no longer necessary to try to escape it, overcome it, attack it, or project it either onto others or onto God.

While the primary prerequisite for adherence to religion is faith, the essential required qualities needed for following the pathway of nonduality are humility, surrender, and devotional dedication to the pathway. It is readily observable that followers of religions are characterized by the presumption of 'I know' via scriptural authority, ecclesiastical doctrine, historical precedent, etc. In contrast, the spiritual devotee of nonduality starts from the basic, more truthful position, "I, of myself, *don't know*." In Christianity, Jesus Christ *is* The Way, and without His help (Grace), the ego (sin) cannot be transcended. Although "heaven is within you," its reality is not realizable without a Savior because of the sheer tenacity of the ego. Thus, Jesus taught the way to salvation. In contrast, the Buddha taught the pathway to Enlightenment, which, however, was not possible to realize without the Grace of the Enlightened Teacher.

The traditional spiritual devotee usually combines the approaches of both faith and self-inquiry. Christianity, Islam, and Judaism emphasize Divinity as Transcendent. The mystics of the world's great traditions focus instead on the Realization of Divinity as Immanent. Whether God is conceived of as transcendental, immanent, or both, is a province of *res interna*, and the realization that God is both immanent and transcendent (*res externa, extensa*) is a consequence of the Realization of the Self and Enlightenment.

Discussion

Q: What is different about the pathway of devotional nonduality compared to traditional teachings?

A: It is characterized by the elimination of all trappings and nonessentials, for time is short and narrow are the gates. It is therefore not pertinent to the past, doctrine, dogma, historical rituals, personages, events, or belief systems. Empowerment is from within by assent of the will. Truth stands forth of its own when the obstacles are removed. The call is from within rather than a response to exhortation from without. The Source is both the initiator as well as the destination. Spiritual information is now available for the first time that, throughout history, has never before been accessible. The capacity to identify truth from falsehood and the degree of its expression is now a major asset and advantage. According to consciousness research, the likelihood of reaching Enlightenment is now approximately one thousand times more likely than it was in the past.

Q: But is not the quest for Enlightenment difficult or even obscure?

A: It is no longer as difficult. There is much greater clarity about the structure, origin, and evolutionary mechanisms of the ego. Its function no longer needs to be obscured by moralistic religious denunciation. Pejorative religious terminology of the ego/mind's evolutionary propensities created intimidation and fearful, guilty resistance, and therefore great reluctance to really look inside oneself. If viewed with clarity, the ego's mechanisms obviously seem to be merely the means for presumptive biological/emotional survival. They served the evolution and survival of the animal body and its primitive mental mechanisms. The ego is now conceived to be primitive rather than evil or demonic. In human-ego psychology, that which is given severely pejorative labels tends to become repressed or at least suppressed, as well as denied, rejected, and projected onto the world, other people, and even onto Divinity.

Such depictions also result in other psychological measures, such as 'opposite formation', excessive attempts at undoing, obsessive guilt, self-condemnation, self-hatred, and seeing oneself as evil, hateful, and unlovable. With a more enlightened view, the ego is merely seen to be needful of correction and transcendence.

Q: Is not the pathway of nonduality arduous?

A: It is not the pathway that is arduous but merely the degree of the ego's resistance to it. This resistance is overcome by invoking the will, which then institutes the spiritual capacities for dedication, effort, and the willingness to surrender obstacles. Devotion invites the power of love by which humility removes the ego's props and positionalities. It also activates the utilization of information that is transformative. Intention energizes willingness, which thereby enables transformation to replace the limitations consequent to resistance. It is only necessary to institute rather simple procedures and processes that could be likened to 'spiritual engineering' by which identifying the structures and forces involved automatically reveals the necessary processes required to undo the basic structural functions.

Q: Example?

A: A person feels trapped by what is believed to be a worldly goal, such as money, fame, or possessions. With analysis, it becomes clear that it is not the 'things' themselves to which one is attracted or attached but primarily the 'juice' or pleasurable emotional gratification attached to them. It is really not 'winning' that is desired or important but the payoff of the juice of emotional satisfaction itself. Thus, the question arises not whether one can relinquish the desire for wealth and fame but 'could one' surrender the 'juice' of the payoff to God. With resistance, the mind may think, "No, I can't," but then if questioned again, "At gunpoint, could you?" the answer is obviously, "Oh, yes." Therefore, the underlying process of resistance is not 'could' but 'would'. 'Can't' implies impossibility, whereas 'don't want to' or 'would' implies that the real, underlying resistance is that of unwillingness.

To surrender a goal does not mean to automatically lose it. What is illusive via greed often effortlessly materializes as a consequence of evolving to a higher level of consciousness. Note that the level of experiential happiness rises in exact accord with the level of consciousness and not with material success.

Q: Why is devotion necessary or important?

A: The mind is often aware of error and character defects, but it lacks the power or incentive to surrender them. Devotion is of the heart and has the strength and motivation to overcome resistances and obstacles beyond the capacity of mere mentalization. An aspect of devotional love is constancy, as well as loyalty and commitment, "no matter what." Devotion includes fortitude and alignment with endeavor and is like the glue that holds all these aspects together.

Devotion is like an inner valor or fortitude that incorporates courage, willingness, and conviction, together with the knowledge of essential information. It develops wisdom, patience, and forbearance with experience. Because of focus, it also develops skill and aptitude for processing the levels of consciousness as they are encountered (as per *Transcending the Levels of Consciousness* [Hawkins, 2006]). Devotion learns to expect periods of delay or discouragement as well as moments of doubt or fear. By virtue of devotion, there is alignment with inner integrity that results in the self-honesty and conviction necessary to transcend the seduction of transitory emotional payoffs of the intransigent ego.

The desire to reach Enlightenment is already a Divine gift to be treasured and revered. "Many are called but few are chosen" could be rephrased as "Many are called but few choose to follow." Thus, the choice is by decision and assent of the inner will, and by this assent, the enormous power of

Divine Will aligns with intention and empowers devotion to overcome all obstacles.

CHAPTER 2

The Inner Path

Introduction

All people live by faith. The only variable is in 'what' that faith is placed. The selection reflects a level of consciousness that, in turn, is correlated with perception, values, and intrinsic capacity for comprehension and primary motivation.

Predominant in human history is alliance with the animal instincts of physical survival and therefore the accumulation of the means to that end. Akin to bodily survival is the seeking of pleasure, which energizes curiosity and eventually thought. Survival is enhanced by group formation as family, tribe, and society, the success of which depends on the development of communication and the organization of relationship.

Discourse arises from the capacity for ideation and language that progress from the concrete, literal, and physical to symbolic abstraction as the capacity for intellection. Eventually, out of curiosity arise the basic existential questions: Who are we? Where did we come from? Where do we go? These are basically the questions of identity as well as of the purpose and meaning of life itself. Thus began the basic surge for a primordial truth by which to contextualize life and extract meaning, significance, and value.

Some people are satisfied with merely the rudimentary mechanics of physical animal pleasure and survival, but over the ages, the majority of mankind has intuited a greater understanding and meaning that have come about via great teachers and spiritual geniuses. Great prophets, sages, and avatars emerged, and their spiritual energy and levels of consciousness were so high that they profoundly influenced and shaped civilization for millennia.

The world's great religions emerged as a major dominant influence over civilizations by providing a greater contextualization of Reality and its derivative expressions as meaning, values, and philosophical formulation that were the basic structure of society and even of government itself. Religions beneficially provided an ethical and moral context for law, social behavior, and organization. Interestingly, some societies, after incorporating the basic structures that arose from religion, such as government and law, eventually formally eliminated the recognition of religions from which they had emerged. Thus, officially secular nations, by virtue of their origination, operate according to religious principles (human rights, equality, morality, ethics, accountability, responsibility, etc.). The core of spiritual truth innate to religion survived as the basic principles of civilization itself.

Discussion

Throughout the history of civilization, mankind has sought to understand the significance of human life, and different cultures have produced a variety of religious as well as philosophical and mythical belief systems. Religions often became dominant theocracies by which values were reinforced through laws and social customs. Common to all religions, however, was the concept of Divinity or spiritual Reality, exemplified by monotheism or a pantheon of gods or dominant spirits whose primary characteristic was power. Thus, Divinity was universally worshipped in various forms by acknowledging sovereignty.

The calibrated level of truth of the various religions over time shows a very wide range, and in some very primitive societies, it calibrated far below level 200, with the religious emphasis on animal, but especially human, sacrifice as well as overt cruelty by which the populace was terrorized (e.g., the Mayan religion calibrated at 95). In comparison, other religions were based on the inspiration of prophets who calibrated well above 200, and yet the religions continued to include ritual sacrifice and subordination of the people. From Abraham arose the three great religions of Christianity, Judaism, and Islam via the great avatars Jesus Christ, Moses, and later, Muhammad. Followers of these great religions became related as "people of the Book," the Sons of Abraham who, unfortunately, subsequently engaged in rivalry and bloodshed.

Approximately five thousand years prior to the emergence of the Semitic religions, the great Aryan sages emerged in ancient India. The influence of these sages is indicated by their extremely high calibrations of levels of truth as exhibited by the *Vedas* and the *Upanishad's* teachings ascribed to Krishna (cal. 1,000). These revelations of spiritual truth are depicted as 'nonlinear' and therefore nondualistic, as were exemplified by the teachings of the Buddha (cal. 1,000), who appeared in approximately 563 B.C. The teachings of Jesus Christ (cal. 1,000) clarified the relationship between God and man, and monotheism was later substantiated and glorified by the teachings of Muhammad (original calibration level 700). Thus, spiritual truth of very high calibrated validity became widely available and spread throughout all human civilization. Even aboriginal societies and civilizations, such as Native

American, spontaneously discovered the Reality of the
Divinity of God and accorded reverence to the Great
Spirit as Creator.

The Contrast Between Nonduality and Traditional Religion

The traditional religions involve the requirement
for learning or even memorizing ecclesiastical religious
doctrines and their historical or mythological origins
and sources, including even times and places, along
with the citation of authority, precedent, and illustrious
figures and contributors. Also included are religious
rules and regulations, as well as proscriptions regarding
lifestyle, dress, hairstyles, etc. In addition, requirements
evolved, such as attendance, membership, and group
commitments. These usually resulted in social/group
inclusions and exclusions that involved group identifications and classifications (e.g., believers versus nonbelievers).

In addition, there emerged rules of conduct and
relationship, including marriage, procreation, and
social and sexual activities based on ecclesiastical
doctrine, correlated with specified ethnic tribal cultures limited in time and geography. By virtue of their
origination, cultural lifestyles became intertwined
with religious teachings that included various interpretations of the actual teachings of the original great
teacher/founder/avatar. Often centuries elapsed
before the teachings, which had been verbally handed
down over time, became translated into written language. The exact, final wording was often somewhat
contentious, and various factions sought dominance
or control; thus, some scriptures were actually arrived
at by virtue of the voting of various groups. Formal

scriptures finally emerged but at a lower calibration level than that of the original teachings. Error was also consequent to misquotes as well as editing by sequential scribes.

Contributing to the decline was the inclusion of extraneous matters that were given importance equal to the essentials. A primary value of traditional religions, however, is that the 'mystical' illuminations of the great founders became languaged and presented in a contextualization that was comprehensible to larger numbers of people who were neither spiritually nor intellectually sophisticated. Therefore, myth and fable often became included for their pedagogical value and appeal. This was of pragmatic value in that it translated the seemingly abstract to the more easily comprehensible concrete, literal exemplifications.

A brilliant distillation of the essential spiritual truths and the world's great religions is exemplified by the following:

1. **Christianity** is the path of love and forgiveness.
2. **Buddhism** is the path of compassion.
3. **Judaism** is the path of living by sacred law.
4. **Baha'i** is the path of unity and peace.
5. **Islam** is the path of submission to the will of God.
6. **Confucianism** is the path of deliberate tradition.
7. **Taoism** is the path of ultimate reality.
8. **Native American Practice** is the path of primal spirituality.
9. **Shintoism** is the path of tribal ancestry.
10. **Hinduism** is the path of knowledge, action, and devotion.
11. **Science of Mind** is the path of the Divine Principle of Love and Law.

12. **The Global Heart Vision** is of a world that
works for everyone.

(Henderson, R., 2005)

Nondualistic Teachings

Concepts and teachings that calibrate below 600
are comprehensible to the majority of people, and the
teachings in the calibration range of the 500s (Love)
have a major influence. Although the perfection of
love to the level of Unconditional Love at calibration
540 is reached by only 0.4 percent of today's overall
world population, it is nonetheless comprehended as a
real, experiential possibility, and exceptional individuals who continue to evolve in consciousness to the
high 500s are termed 'saints,' thereby serving as models
for humanity as a practical goal. The spiritual ecstasy of
the very high 500s is also recorded (e.g., Ramakrishna
or the great Christian saints) and thereby given credence and acceptance as a possible reality for those
who are exceptionally motivated or gifted.

At consciousness level 500, there is a major shift of
paradigm, and from consciousness level 600 and up,
the spiritual reality is described as ineffable or mystical.
Its nondual quality (i.e., 'no mind', or 'Mind') makes
such a condition difficult to language or conceptualize
and therefore seemingly limited as an actual experiential
possibility. Advanced students are familiar with the
writings of the great sages whose work is characterized
by the Sanskrit terms *Advaita* and *Vedanta*, about
which there is considerable information available
through the writings of recent well-known teachers,
such as Ramana Maharshi or Nisargadatta Maharaj. On

a similar level are the teachings of great, well-known mystics of all religions, such as the Sufis, the Kabbalah, or the Zohar. Of major importance, and also well known, are the teachings of the Buddha, the Hindu sages, and the Zen adepts. Credence as to the actuality and reality of Enlightenment is supported by the rather extensive literature about such states by well-known scholars, such as William James, and later scholars of the Zen tradition, such as D. T. Suzuki and Alan Watts.

The difficulty in describing or explaining such states is simply that the consciousness level of the intellect is limited to the 400s and includes the presumption of cause and effect. Despite the descriptions, the states themselves are nonlinear and thus can be alluded to but not accurately described in familiar language. Despite the limitation of accurate depiction, the reality of such states is universally recognized, and most recently, such states have been validated by calibrated levels of consciousness research, which confirms the Reality of enlightened states of consciousness. Despite their statistical rarity, such advanced states are inspirational and give recognition to the potential of human consciousness to evolve.

The fact that the enlightened condition is not comprehensible, explicable, or possible of 'acquisition' by the mind/intellect dismays spiritual seekers; thus, such states may seem unreachable and therefore not practical as a goal. On the contrary, in actuality, advanced states are powerfully experiential because the Reality that they confirm and reflect is already a fact consequent to the very obvious actuality that one already 'exists'. Thus, every spiritual student already has met the primordial requisite quality, and it is only necessary to add motivation and commitment. Thus, the only requirements are, first, to exist, then to have heard of enlightenment, and then to seek it as a realizable goal. What makes it seem difficult is the dearth of simple information and clarification, for experientially the way is innately simple, although at times seemingly arduous.

Another reason that reaching the state of Enlightenment seems impractical is because the mind conceptualizes in terms of cause and effect, and students conceive of themselves as being driven (i.e., implying inner will power, etc.) instead of the reality that they are actually being attracted by their future destiny.

Comfort and confidence can be derived from a verifiable reality that the rare persons who are actually attracted to Enlightenment as a life goal are attracted because that is already their destiny (calibrates as true). For the same reason, only future golfers would be taking golf lessons.

Q: How does the inner pathway differ from traditional religious observance?

A: The emphasis is on the inner experiential subjective realization and internal validation of spiritual truth. In contrast, religion is formalized and historically structured in an authoritative context that stresses conformation to observances, rituals, customs, and belief systems. Thereby, the origination of truth is projected backwards in time to other cultures, places, and ethnic circumstances. In addition, there is also emphasis on mystification, glorification, and dramatization, intermingled with theological doctrine. In religion, Divinity is contextualized primarily as elsewhere in time and location and is also described as having human motivations, limitations, and defects. Religion emphasizes belief rather than the inner realization of truth. In religion, there is also a major emphasis on spiritual destiny in the future after physical death rather than on the experiencing of spiritual truth in the present.

Q: What personality characteristics are favorable for the inner pathway?

A: Characteristically, devotees tend to be introspective, thoughtful, reflective, curious, responsible, and attentive. There is usually an aversion to violence, cruelty, nonintegrity, and the fanfare and drama of glamour or vulgarity. There are the attraction to learning for its own sake and the pleasure of discovery of basic premises.

Q: What of the demands of daily life?

A: The inner path is a way of continuously being with oneself and life in the world, whereas religious observance tends to become compartmentalized. Spiritual devotion is a continuous inner lifestyle that incorporates constant watchful awareness. External occurrences are transitory, whereas inner qualities of consciousness are more permanent. Inner work is a constant learning process whereby there are pleasure and satisfaction in discovery and the unfolding of insight. The process is self-rewarding and, paradoxically, this results in greater benefit and enjoyment of formal religious participation or practices as well.

The reflections of truth are everywhere to be seen and recognized in multitudinous expressions. By internal observation, there develops an inner wisdom that facilitates compassion and spiritual comprehension rather than an 'ought to' discipline. With inner awareness, religious guilt and preoccupation with sin diminish, and instead, one chooses positive options rather than being controlled by negative programs resulting in shame, fear, and guilt.

Fulfillment of potential is rewarding and gratifying, which in turn progressively reinforces motivation. Self-honesty brings greater inner freedom as well as adaptational expertise and flexibility. It is not necessary to withdraw from the world but instead to recontextualize it. Spiritual evolution results in greater capability due to the advancement of consciousness that ensues. It is a matter of motivation. It is not necessary to go into monastic retreat, although there may be such periods that are beneficial.

Q: What is a workable goal?
A: To verify spiritual truth experientially and to become it rather than just conform to it. The process is an unfolding of discovery resulting in greater happiness and diminution of fear, guilt, and other negative emotions. The motive is inner development, evolution, and fulfillment of potential, which is independent of the external world. Life becomes progressive rather than just repetitive. All experience is of equal value

and innately pleasurable so that life stops being an endless sequence of alternating pleasure and displeasure. With inner progress, context expands, resulting in greater awareness of significance and meaning, and therefore, gratification of potential.

Q: **Inner spiritual work seems to require discipline and endeavor.**

A: These requirements are activated by intention. There is an innate gratification in spiritual growth and the evolution of consciousness itself. Progress is the consequence of clarification and greater understanding that arise from the expansion of context. Recontextualization then results in transcending the distortions of perception.

Q: **Inner work concerns focus rather than specific, special activity?**

A: The average person is focused on participating successfully in the world and its activities via education, success, relationships, etc. The inner work, 'to know thyself', is focused on inner comprehension of life events, including expectations, motives, attitudes, and habitual thought patterns. Curiosity arises: "Why do I see that situation the way I do?" or, "Why do I feel as I do? What is my prevailing attitude, and what programs are actually running my mind?" These questions lead to an interesting discovery of prevailing presumptions about oneself, life, and others. Prevailing goals and values become apparent for examination as well as the degree to which they are prioritized.

Q: That brings up the quote, "The unexamined life is not worth living."

A: Although the quotation might seem to be somewhat of an overstatement, it does contain a valuable truth and observation, which is also validated by the premises of quantum mechanics (the Heisenberg principle) in that observation itself changes outcome as a consequence of not only the introduction of the field of consciousness but also its intention.

To a highly aware person, most people seem to walk about as if they are in some kind of a dream state, unconscious and unaware of themselves. Self-observation leads to awakening, which then motivates the desire to learn, grow, mature, and evolve. Self-inquiry leads to discovery and the unfolding of the layers that obscure the Self. With self-inquiry, one examines the basis for faith and beliefs, and by instituting spiritual techniques and criteria, proceeds to discover the inner validation of spiritual truths for oneself. Thus, the field of inquiry is the function of consciousness/awareness and the manner in which it contextualizes the inner experience of self, others, and Divinity.

There is a difference between having 'heard' a truth and having discovered it as an inner reality. The way to 'be it' is to own it as an experiential reality.

Q: But is that not what is called 'solipsism'?

A: Solipsism is an intellectual belief that only the subjective experience of the self is 'real'. Thus, people live in different subjective realities. Solipsism is valid up to a point as it applies to the ego/self, i.e., each person lives within their own perceptual version of reality. In contrast, this limitation is transcended by the very process of inner spiritual work, which progresses to the elimination of the limitations of perception (i.e., the world of illusion), so as to reveal the Reality of the Self.

CHAPTER 3

Orientation

Introduction

Spiritual evolution is supported by education and information up to the point where the intellect is no longer a primary tool as it is in ordinary learning. The spiritual 'work' then transitions from the mental/intellectual/conceptual linear to the nonlinear region of human consciousness, which relates more to context than to content and form or data. The transition is from the specific content to the quality of subjective experiencing itself. This major shift entails reliance on different qualities, such as faith, intention, devotion, volition, and the will. Character traits are called into action, and attitudes are of greater practical use than specific ideas.

Whereas ordinary information is 'acquired' by effort, in spiritual endeavor the emphasis is on relinquishing, letting go, and surrendering. The 'work' involves identifying positionalities and then transcending the ego's resistances and relinquishing its illusory control or sovereignty.

Thus, the core of spiritual work is aligned with undoing and the unloading of the mind rather than its enrichment. To seek Enlightenment is a major decision. The decision itself is therefore akin to a 'Yang' position, but subsequently, the process itself is more intrinsically akin to a 'Yin' posture. While the ordinary ego is programmed to 'getting', spiritual intention now shifts to 'allowing', similar to floating in the water rather than flailing about or swimming in it. The actual process is innately simple yet challenging of accomplishment by virtue of the innate structure of the ego/mind, which resists loss of dominion by inventing a plethora of arguments and defenses. Another resistance is that ordinary mind dislikes taking responsibility, even for very trivial matters. (For example, "Who forgot to lock the screen door?" "Not me; it must have been the dog.")

Posture

The spiritual practice of seeking Enlightenment via nonduality is the consequence of intention and commitment. Its actual practice is not so much a matter of 'doing' but a way of 'being' or aligning with the subjective awareness of life. It is therefore like a posture as represented, for example, by the classic *mudra* (sacred hand position). Attention is aligned with the field/context rather than the customary focus on content and details. Intuition is valuable and investigative rather than being dismissed as illogical. Also, spiritual work is more like noticing and becoming aware rather than 'doingness' per se.

Attitudes that may just seem merely 'nice' to ordinary mind become very powerful tools when aligned with spiritual intention and commitment. For instance, to strictly live by the dictum of 'good will to all life' is transformative when energized by the Spiritual Will. The decisions to 'be kind to all of life' or to respect the sacredness of all that exists are powerful attitudes in spiritual evolution, along with the virtues of compassion, the willingness to forgive, and seeking to understand rather than to judge. By constant surrendering, perceptions dissolve into discernment of essence.

Supplication and prayer to Divinity are facilitated by a profound and deep surrender to humility. This humility is merely the truthful acknowledgment of the actual fact that the ego/mind, by virtue of its structure and design, is intrinsically incapable of being able to differentiate truth from falsehood (essence from appearance). Emotion is not an indicator of truth as it is both reflective and determinative of positionalities and conditioning.

It is important to realize that both the level of consciousness and karmic propensities are consequences of prior acts of the will. In contrast, in ordinary worldly life, rewards are based on gain and demonstration of accomplishments or acquisitions. Surrender and humility are not the same thing as passivity because, paradoxically, both surrender and humility are positive acts of the Spiritual Will and are thereby in a positive agreement to 'allow' rather than to 'get'.

Focus

In ordinary life, the mind focuses on linear content, specific details, and emotionalized perception. The ego is thus energized consequent to projected, inflated estimates of worth or value. The process of energizing perceptions and desires is based on the ego's expectations of gratification and reward. In contrast, in spiritual endeavor, the focus is not on the result but instead on alignment with an overall field of intention.

The ego is oriented towards specifics and the linear content of the field of vision. Its effect on vision itself is exclusive and limited in order to focus primarily on the near side of objects (so as to facilitate manipulation). Spirit is oriented towards context and the whole, and is thus inclusive and focuses on the far side of objects. Its field is diffuse rather than local.

To relate to the overall field rather than become involved in the details of specifics is characteristic of a contemplative lifestyle, which is conducive to spiritual evolution. In meditative practice also, there is a shift from focus on specifics at the outset but then progressive identification with the overall field and eventually with context itself.

When vision is focused on a desired object, the focus is on the near side of the object. In contrast, looking at what or who is loved results in the inclusive shift of focus to the far side.

In ordinary life, the ego/mind goes from 'unfinished' to 'finished', and then from 'incomplete' to 'complete'. In contrast, the spiritual pathway is a direction and style that goes from complete to complete as evolutionary states of emergence. Ego positions are interactive and usually represent a composite. For example, to disassemble anger may require the willingness to surrender the pride that underlies that anger, which in turn depends on surrendering a desire. This means surrendering the fear that energized the desire, which again is related to the undoing of imaginary loss, and so forth. Motivations are thus intertwined and mutually interactive, and operationally surrendering them leads to the next levels, which are comprised of dualities. The deeper layers, therefore, tend to surface one's beliefs about God, programmed spiritual expectations, and belief systems. Spiritual work is therefore a matter of exploration that transcends mentalized concepts, such as those of cause and effect.

It is helpful to understand that a specific level of consciousness is aligned with an 'attractor field' that, like a magnet, attracts similarities. Although the personal self likes to think that the thoughts going through the mind are 'my thoughts', they are actually only 'the thoughts' that prevail at a given level of consciousness. It is like different depths in the sea attract different types of fish. Thus, if one's calibrated level of consciousness is primarily in the field of pride, then the field itself impersonally attracts similar supportive thoughts that are quite different from the ones that prevail with an overall attitude of neutrality or acceptance.

Spiritual intention subserves, reinforces, and focuses on witnessing and observing rather than on doingness or specifics. Spiritual processing is like positioning oneself in the wind or in a water current.

Spiritual motivation, intention, and alignment could be likened to changing the magnetic or gravitational field of influence by which context is shifted, revealing a different understanding. For example, a presumed loss becomes recontextualized as a hidden gain (greater freedom, opening of opportunities and choices, etc.). By comparison, from the level of Pride, the options are few and limited, but from Willingness, Surrender, and Acceptance, the options are multitudinous.

The Will

The Spiritual Will is not like the ego's understanding of will as 'will power', which means emotional force with clenched teeth of exertion and increased emotionality. The ego-driven will takes energy and is taxing. It could actually be understood as a form of aggression. In contrast, invoking the Spiritual Will is like opening floodgates and then standing back. The ego/will contextualizes events in terms of cause and effect in which the personal self-will claims credit or blame because it sees itself as a causal agent. In contrast, the Spiritual Will is not personal but is a quality of consciousness that changes context by surrender to an invitation to the power of the Self. The Spiritual Will calibrates at 850, and the personal will calibrates at only the person's current level of consciousness.

The Spiritual Will, invited by complete surrender, is thus capable of performing the seeming 'miraculous', whereas the personal will, paradoxically, often automatically triggers resistances, as anyone knows who has tried personal 'will power' to overcome even minor habits.

Surrender of the personal will to the Will (Wisdom) of God (or Providence, Higher Power) signifies relinquishment of control. One can expect the ego to resist doing so, and it invents excuses, counterarguments, and multiple fears in order to maintain illusory control. The ego's positions are reinforced by pride as well as desire for specific results. Thus, to the ego, to step back and invite the intervention of Divinity seems like a loss, whereas, to the Spirit, it is definitely a win.

Another limitation of the personal will is that it has no knowledge of karmic propensities or propitious timing, nor does it have the wisdom (omnipotence) to comprehend beneficial sequence. The Self orchestrates with an inner knowingness of capacity. For instance, to try to face a certain conflict prematurely may be unsuccessful, whereas it would have been successful after a few other layers of the conflict had been resolved.

Alignment of Awareness

Spiritual alignment is with context rather than content. To watch the mind is far different from identifying with it. To witness and observe are beneficially removed from the alternative of emotional involvement and gain-or-loss participation in the world of perception. To watch the mind from a detached position is educational, nonstressful, and can be done with equanimity. Whereas the consciousness level of the witness/observer increases awareness, the ego watches with the expectation of 'doing' or 'getting' something. With the style of detached observation, the unfolding of life reveals itself to be the consequence of the spontaneous emergence of actuality as a manifestation of potentiality when conditions are favorable.

By the practice of nonattachment (as compared to detachment), the spectator viewpoint can be maintained even during participation because the spectator learns 'about' an event but is not 'of it'. Nonattachment becomes possible with relinquishment of the desires for gain. With deep surrender and continued alignment, identification with awareness eventually disappears along with the loss of identification with the witness/observer/watcher. The Self is innately complete unto itself and is therefore not needful nor is it subject to the positionalities of subject/object. The field is independent of content. Consciousness just *is*, with no stakes in the unfoldment of Creation. Eventually, the autonomous spontaneity whereby potentiality unfolds as Creation reveals that Evolution and Creation are one and the same thing.

Q: Spiritual inquiry starts with acquired information derived from study, etc. This then results in the obstacle of the mind's conclusion that "I know." How can valid information

be held so as not to create the obstacle of presumption?

A: To the seeker of the truth of the inner pathway of nonduality, all learning is held as tentative until the innate truth reveals itself and is validated experientially. This process is potentiated by recontextualization. Classically, the recommended position from which to hold information is clarified by the phrase "So I have heard," which implies the holding back of transferring information into a belief system. That information has become an integrated 'knowingness' is indicated by a transformational change of perception consequent to full understanding. This is often the result of reflection and contemplation.

Q: **Can you amplify that with an example?**

A: Both the Buddha and Jesus Christ taught that the basic 'sin' (defect) of humans is ignorance. Socrates taught that all men are intrinsically innocent because they always choose what they perceive to be the good, even though it is in error. A Course in Miracles teaches that everyone is intrinsically innocent and merely beguiled by the ego. Thus, sin means limitation, error, and misperception due to the impaired capacity. It also represents the limitation of evolution.

Consciousness research indicates that the human ego/mind is constitutionally unable to differentiate truth from falsehood by virtue of its construction. The mind is like the hardware of a computer that will play back anything for which it has been programmed, whether it be propaganda, misinformation, emotional distortion, bias, fallacious memes (slogans), etc.

To fully 'know' a reality is to 'be' it, which is a transformative absorption and full integration. Complete acceptance would therefore result in the termination of judgmentalism, anger, resentment, blame, guilt, and hatred of self and others. Full acceptance, on the other hand, does not mean becoming an apologist for grossly negative, destructive behavior. A bull may misperceive a bystander as a potential enemy, but that does not mean that one thereby allows oneself to be needlessly gored.

Spirituality is often confused with passivity. Moral obligation to respect and honor life includes one's own as well. Truth is strength as an expression of integrity. Moral stance is not the same as physical action, which, in and of itself, is neutral. The consciousness calibration level of an action is determined by intention. With progression of the evolution of consciousness, there arises the capacity for the Tao of the 'non-action of action,' which is indicative of mastery and exemplified by the martial arts. Culpability is aligned with capability and actual possibility. It is akin to situational ethics, which includes overall context as well as content.

Q: **Many spiritual and moral dilemmas therefore cannot be resolved within just the limited level of content.**

A: That is a clear observation. Even just adding historical and cultural context already alters the appearance of many phenomena. To understand the evolutionary origins of the ego itself and its alignment with the support of animal evolutionary life creates a more comprehensive, expanded paradigm from which to view human motivation and behavior.

Available options are limited by the level of consciousness and vary quite differently from one level to another. This realization also facilitates compassion instead of judgmentalism.

Much judgmentalism arises from posing the hypothetical, i.e., that people 'should' be different; however, if they could be, they would be. The hypothetically possible becomes actual by intention as well as the level of evolution of consciousness plus favorable conditions.

One of the most important operational conditions that limits options and not available to ordinary perception is karmic patterns, including propensities and unresolved obligations, as well as the presentation of karmic opportunities.

Q: What does 'karma' mean? Is it not just a belief system?

A: Karma really means the totality of one's inheritance, which includes both the known and the unknown, both the linear and the nonlinear. To just be born a human being already represents the expression of untold millions of factors. Genes or chromosomes are merely the mechanisms of karmic transmission that already include the mechanics of physicality, the expression of which requires enormous informational patterns.

Everyone already has a calibratable level of consciousness at the moment of birth that is thereby correlated with physicality itself. The

Western world accepts karmic consequences subsequent to physical death as the destiny of the soul. The Eastern world accepts the reality of karma as an ongoingness of the evolution of the spirit over great periods of time. Consciousness calibration confirms and extensively demonstrates that every intention or action, even in its most minute details, is embedded and recorded forever within the infinite field of consciousness. It is also confirmable (at consciousness level 1,000) that everyone, without exception, is accountable to the Universe (i.e., the Mind of God or Divine Providence alluded to by whatever term chosen). Thus arises the wisdom that "God is not mocked," and that "Every hair on one's head is numbered."

Q: But are not many characteristics or events just accidental?

A: The infinite eternal field of the Unmanifest becomes Manifest as Creation by virtue of Divine Ordinance (as an expression of its essence). The power of the field is absolute and inclusive, all present and beyond time, and within it, manifestation occurs when conditions are favorable. Intention itself is also a contributing factor.

There are no possibilities outside the infinite realm of Reality because all possibilities have already been included within Creation itself. The term 'accidental' is a hypothetical absurdity, like proving that a physical object on planet earth is not subject to the laws of gravity. Even the concept of 'chaos' means unpredictable from a limited, linear Newtonian or mathematical viewpoint. Reason, logic, and predictability are limited to the consciousness levels of the 400s, whereas Reality has no such limitations or restraints. All comes into actualization from potentiality, and the laws of karma are not only linear but also contextualized via the nonlinear as well.

Chaos is a mentalization that implies unidentifiable and unpredictable, which means not identifiable or predictable from a linear, mathematical viewpoint, that is, no identifiable pattern. Context is local and identifiable, as well as nonlocal and unidentifiable. Knowability is a reflection of paradigm, which is identifiable by the consciousness calibration of the overall contextual field itself. The real reason much information is not available is because there is a lack of capability to ask the correct question.

Q: Does the inner path require erudition?
A: No. Merely simple attitudes and the necessary motivation are required. To strive to know God is in itself pristine and the ultimate aspiration.

CHAPTER 4

Spiritual Practices

Introduction

Human ingenuity has resulted in a great variety and number of spiritual practices, many of which were listed and calibrated in Chapter 17 of *Truth vs. Falsehood.* Each has its historic roots that include ethnic and cultural proclivities as well as practices that are aligned with specific belief systems. Many practices are quite imaginative rituals, and their consciousness calibration level indicates that their benefit arises primarily from the spiritual intention with which they are done rather than from the practice itself. Therefore, it is said that there are "ten thousand ways to God," for each practice fulfills a purpose at a given time in each individual's spiritual evolution.

Some practices are almost universal in their expression, such as devotion and worship of Divinity by whatever designation. In contrast, some practices are quite unique to the degree that they become imbued with mysticism and magic. These often involve entreaty and/or manipulation of various linear energy fields and the invoking of unseen spirits. These practices actually rely on techniques of magic and typically calibrate quite low, frequently below the consciousness level of truth at 200.

The major genuine spiritual practices include individual and group worship and prayer, including music, incense, creative arts, and dance, as well as symbols, postures, and *mudra.* These are often associated with styles of dress, dietary observances, genuflections, bodily prostration, fasting, prayer beads, and the rhythmic chanting of mantras. Group activities reflect not only worship but also gratitude to Divinity for life and its expressions of God's Grace. In daily life, formal prayer of gratitude is most commonly 'saying Grace' before meals, the benefit of which is corroborated by consciousness calibration research, which shows that the actual energy of the food itself increases by ten to twenty points.

In all societies, the prudent acknowledge God, even if they personally harbor doubts or lack conviction. The universality of the acknowledgment of Divinity throughout time in all cultures and in all ages represents the intuitive awareness and wisdom within the collective consciousness of all of mankind, which is independent of locality or time frame.

Some practices include the intention of influencing God in a desired direction for some specific benefit. Other practices are intended to assuage what are believed to be the negative depictions of God and therefore include personal or ritual sacrifice, as well as that of animals or humans. Thus, even killing life itself has been incorporated into rituals that in themselves calibrate extremely low, indicating very serious and sizeable error and deviation from truth.

The calibration level of a spiritual practice reflects the degree to which it is actually intrinsically aligned with spiritual truth rather than illusion and imagination. Because Divinity is nonlinear and intangible, God is the ultimate screen upon which to project the endless errors and proclivities of the human ego. Thus, Divinity is often depicted as having a distinct personality. The Presence of God as Creator is intuited by mankind, and the infinite nonlinear Reality that is the very source of all of Creation and

Existence is present within the discrete linear domain as the Source of its Existence. This is reflected in the Roman Catholic ecclesiastical doctrine of "The Natural Law" which states that humankind is created with the capacity to realize God as Creator, and therefore, there is the moral obligation to do so. (The Natural Law doctrine calibrates at 570.) This is an accepted realty by approximately 90 to 92 percent of Americans currently.

The universality of Divinity is acknowledged in all major religions, such as the Hindu pantheon or the Christian Trinity. It also appears in the Hindu religion as the trinity of Vishnu, Shiva, and Brahma. There are also diverse depictions of various expressions of the Buddha, and Krishna is also envisioned in different roles. In the monotheism of Christian or Judaic theology, God is conceptualized as primarily transcendent. Consciousness calibration research confirms that God is transcendent, immanent, and present in all that exists as the very Source of Existence itself, and thus the non-linear is simultaneously present in the linear.

The prominent form of spiritual practice that prevails in the majority of the world's religions is the repetition of scripture or portions of verse that are also frequently the basis for instructional teaching via sermons or study groups. Also common to all religions are group practices, such as pilgrimages, retreats, and religious festivals and celebrations, and symbols of Divinity depicted allegorically in form as statues, graphics, spiritually inspired monuments, stupas, and pyramids. Even traversing patterns, such as the geometric arrangement of the labyrinth in the floor of Chartres Cathedral in France, are utilized to increase spiritual awareness. In contrast, Islam, Judaism, and some branches of Eastern Orthodox Christianity eschew icons or depictions of Divinity.

Of considerable interest has been a variety of spiritual practices in the form of repetitious physical exercises, such as the various yogas that also include breathing patterns in a variety of practices designed to control physical and spiritual energy systems via the chakra system. The Grand Yogas all calibrate extremely high and include the selfless service of Karma Yoga (cal. 915), Bhakti (cal. 935), Raja (cal. 935), Kundalini (cal. 510), Kriya (cal. 410), and Hatha (cal. 390). Jhana yoga denotes the pathway of Advaita, or nonduality (cal. 975), which emphasizes meditation and contemplation and is the pathway of the Buddha and great mystics of history.

Included in many religions is also the practice of mantras, or repetitious phrases or prayers, that often emphasize very specific sounds (such as the famous "Om"), or the repetition of the names for God. The downside of repetitious, rhythmic physical chanting and practices is the induction of an artificially altered state of consciousness that may be misidentified as a mystical condition, such as *satori*. On the other hand, however, it may precipitate sudden flashes of insight or peak experiences whose value can best be determined by their subjective impact indicated by an elevation of the level of consciousness or advance in spiritual awareness.

In practice, most spiritual seekers sooner or later investigate a variety of techniques and practices, especially during the initial period of exploration. Most often, the result is allegiance to several practices simultaneously that are compatible with personality, lifestyle, prior spiritual experience, and one's level of consciousness. Also, spiritual doubt may arise along the pathway, which may even express as atheism or agnosticism for periods of time as the search for truth can find multitudinous expressions and go through various seemingly contradictory phases. If inner alignment is with integrity, and inner honesty prevails, the outcome is aligned with the prevailing intention. In the long run, the ultimate guide is actually the inner Self, which, it is commonly believed, is quite happy to throw one bodily off a cliff if that is what it takes to awaken and activate the spirit. The pathway of nonduality is also denoted as Advaita, Jhana yoga, Zen, and, paradoxically, the way via mind to the 'no mind' of Mind.

Devotion intensifies whatever pathway or practices are chosen, and devotion and inner prayer characterize the mystic. The serious, dedicated search for Enlightenment is energized by intention and empowered by devotion, which leads to the inner search for truth characterized by meditation and a contemplative lifestyle. Although, in the beginning, the search may be investigative or even experimental, as time goes on, it becomes the predominant motif and core of one's life as a prevailing dedication.

Meditation

Focused, concentrated introspection can be both peaceful and fulfilling but also quite frustrating. There is an enormous amount of literature on the subject, with descriptions of available techniques and traditions, the most prevalent of which arise from Hindu, Sufi, and Buddhist traditions, as well as from Christian mystics and contemplatives.

To sit cross-legged and unmoving is a learned discipline. The overall purpose is to transcend identification with the body/mind as the self and thus to Realize Self, which is beyond yet inclusive of both.

Most practitioners complain that the mind is ceaseless in its activities. There is an endless sequence of thoughts, concepts, ideas, images, memories, feelings, and anticipations that flow across the mental television screen as an uncontrolled phantasmagoria of random activity.

The intent of meditation is detachment, especially detachment from the notion that the thoughts are 'mine' or represent 'me'. In reality, they are merely 'it's', as is the mind itself. The idea of ownership arises from the personalization of these thoughts due to familiarity because the mind/camera was present to record these past thoughts, events, and memories. However, it recorded them only because they were imbued with importance. Note that little roadside detail is recalled from a boring cross-country drive. The mind's inner television set records what is valued. That which was considered unimportant was not recorded.

Recall and rerun are also the consequence of imagined, projected value. Basically, with examination, it will turn out that the only real value is that they are 'mine'. Thus, just an ordinary shoe is not really noticed, but 'my shoe' is now imbued with value and is therefore remembered.

How much anything is valued can be determined from the emotional response to real or imagined loss. Once thoughts, like objects, are depersonalized, they become devalued and lose their attraction. Thoughts and feelings arise from desire, and the mind desires what it values.

To clear the mind, merely note that nothing at all is of special or unique 'value' or 'worth' except by invested, superimposed, and projected belief. Therefore, withdraw value, worth, importance, and interest.

Q: Is that not a contradiction to the spiritual assumption that all is equally holy and sacred by virtue of the Divinity of its Creation?

A: That 'all is sacred and holy' is, at this stage, merely a belief system of the mind and a repetition of what has been heard. The fact that it is intrinsically a truth reveals itself later without the superimposition of conceptualization. Value, from the ego's viewpoint, is an emotionalized mentalization, and Reality does not require mentalization. With humility, one can integrously state and witness that everything merely 'is as it is', independent of projected worth. Its intrinsic 'value' is that it 'is', i.e., existence is complete within itself and is not needful of projected nominalization as 'special'. When the Divine Essence of All of Creation shines forth without obstruction, then the ego/mind goes silent in awe.

Q: How can the mind be silenced?

A: Ninety-nine percent of the mind is already silent and without linear content. Only one percent is active (as proven by consciousness calibration research), but that one percent is the focus of attention. Note by close observation that each thought arises from a silent, clear field of energy that is the source of thinkingness, ideas, and images. It does not arise, as the mind presumes, as a result of linear causation. On the contrary, each thought arises independently of all the others, like flying fish flying out of the ocean. The ocean is like the silent, primary, a priori condition of the mind and thoughts. The concept that they are somehow caused or meaningfully correlated is actually a superimposed afterthought. Each flying fish arises independently of the others out of primordial still-ness. Interpretation or meaning is via the observer who, for example, upon seeing three fish jump out of the water simultaneously, says, "Look how the fish are triangulating." The mind translates phenomena in 1/10,000th of a second; thus, the mind is like the playback monitor of a tape recorder. When that interface of mind between phenomena and experiencing dissolves, the difference is quite dramatic.

Q: **But what about the classical spiritual teaching of "the space between two thoughts"?**

A: It is a misunderstanding for there is no detectable space 'between' two thoughts through which one can glimpse the Infinite. The supposed 'space' is not between the thoughts but prior to the thoughts.

Perception moves at the same rate as does mentalization; therefore, to expect that perception will discern a space between two thoughts is impossible because perception would have to then move faster than 1/10,000th of a second, that is, the perceptive faculty of the mind moves at the same rate as the content of the mind. Thus, to try to witness the space between two thoughts is like a dog's trying to chase its own tail. This is why many serious and committed meditators do not reach Enlightenment, even after many years of devoted meditation. They are simply looking in the wrong place (calibrates as true).

Q: **Then how can one silence the mind?**

A: One cannot. It stops of its own accord when the energy of interest is removed. It is of greater service to merely disown it and stop identifying with it as 'my mind'. Thoughts are the automatic consequence of a specific calibrated level of consciousness plus personalization by which they gain value. With relinquishment of the activation of memory, one lives in the emergent instant rather than hanging on to the past or anticipating the future.

Q: **To withdraw the magical value of ownership and the concept of 'mine' silences the mind?**

A: It stops when it is not narcissistically energized. Thoughts, ideas, and concepts are of pragmatic and useful value to worldliness, but with the relinquishment of worldliness, they are excess baggage and of no value. In the infinite stillness of a great forest, of what value is a portable radio? One can visit the great, magnificent cathedrals of Europe and witness visitors busily talking on their cell phones and completely missing the wonderment of the stark, stunning beauty. They seem to be walking about unconsciously in some kind of dream world, oblivious to the timeless and silent beauty and magnificence.

Again, the mind stops when it is no longer

narcissistically energized. Thinkingness is intrinsically a vanity. Survival is spontaneous and autonomous, an automatic karmic consequence. Even when the mind becomes totally silent, the body goes about its business like a karmic wind-up toy.

Q: What about meditation on an image or concept?

A: That is focused attention on the linear; however, eventually the mind gets out of the way of the non-linear, and greater meaning then springs forth because it is unobstructed. Formal meditation holding a Divine image in mind is a form of worship and supplication. By surrender and invocation, a knowingness arises via attunement to the teacher's etheric spiritual energy and the consciousness level of the vibrational field. Thus, an image can be inspirational and uplifting, but eventually, that, too, has to be given up as a dependence.

Q: What is the value of mantras?

A: They are in accord with all the above. The purpose is to still the mind and invoke a high energy field. The calibrated levels of various mantras are listed in Chapter 17 of *Truth vs. Falsehood*. For greater benefit, the sound should be held silently.

There is an inherent limitation to repetitious mantras in that they too often result in a semi-auto-hypnotic, altered state of consciousness that actually becomes an obstruction to the sought-for state of Realization. Enlightenment is not an altered state of consciousness induced by alpha waves, feedback, or rhythmic repetitions of dance, sound, breathing, or body movements. It is not the 'high' of drumming, music, bells, chanting, or ascetic extremism. All the above are transitory. When the stomping feet, drums, bells, incense, gongs, and flashing lights stop, so does the artificially induced trance state, which is an altered state of consciousness rather than a Knowingness. Psychedelics also allow glimpses of states of advanced awareness, but they, too, recede.

States of spiritual joy and ecstasy occur naturally at the calibrated levels of the high 500s. To reach Enlightenment, they also must be surrendered to God, and in their place arises a great Peace beyond all description. The Peace of God experientially transcends all prior states, as exquisite as they might have been.

Meditation
Q: What should one focus on in meditation?
A: There are three basic styles that can be described that are effective and fruitful. The first could be described as psychological insight or self-examination. The second is through the thought field, and the third is the simplest by which to bypass the thought field.

Style 1: Psychological
The purpose is focused on understanding and investigating inner motives, attitudes, presumptions, and hidden feelings. This has historically been called self-examination, spiritual inventory, or self-assessment designed to 'know thyself'. The requisite is strong commitment to inner honesty and relinquishment of self-judgment. This reveals the

instinctual drives and their emotional and psychological components. These are then processed through forgiveness, acceptance, and recontextualization.

Style 2: Through the Mind

Look for the energy field of silent stillness, which is ever present and 'situated' just prior to and beneath the advent of thought. Look for the energy source out of which thoughts arise. Watch how a thought begins to arise as a vague kind of feelingness. Progressive specificity then develops. For example, a thought may start out as a general feeling of 'dogginess', and then it specifically evolves into 'a dog'. Next, it quickly particularizes as 'Rover'. Then arises the thought of 'Good old Rover', followed by the sad story of Rover and how he got lost one day, and so on.

By sharp focus and declining involvement, the capacity develops to sharply witness the formation of thought earlier and earlier in the thought-formation process prior to its becoming concretized and linear in defining a specificity. By the above process, attention will be led to the silent, nonlinear origin of the energy field of thinkingness itself. This is the energy field of the desire to think, which is highly prized by the ego, for it is related to the belief/concept of 'I' or 'me'. Thus, it has a creative urgency as a 'need to think' or 'have to think', and the mind flails around in panic to grab a thought in order to survive.

One can surrender the desire of thinkingness to God, which then quickly brings up the mind's fear of survival. At that point, one has to surrender the will to survive to God. If one stops thinking, there is the fear of being mindless. To be thoughtless is called 'Divine idiocy', or 'Divine stupidity'. However, what actually needs to be known will reveal itself, not as thoughts but as comprehension, understanding, and apperception via totalities. The Infinite Reality is omniscient and independent of talkingness, thinkingness, and verbalization of words. The narcissistic ego is addicted to talkingness. It is of no value to the Self. The ego/mind believes that if it stops thinking/feeling, the personal self will die for it is intrinsic to the ego's survival system. Therefore, it fears and avoids silence and stillness. The ego/self identifies with that which is linear, discrete, separate, and definable, i.e., content.

Style 3: Bypassing the Mind
Whereas Styles 1 and 2 are educative, Style 3 is purely subjective/experiential and not mental, psychological, emotional, or conceptual. It is the most rapid and basic and consists of a simple 'doingness'. The steps are very simple: relax completely and deeply; close the eyes; witness the visual field and merely focus on what is witnessed. Within the darkness, notice numerous tiny bits of dancing light phenomena (called "phosgenes"). Become at one with the lights (thoughtlessness ensues), and merge with the visual field. In due time, the context simultaneously begins to shift and deepen. The seeming separation between the witness and the observer disappears. One 'becomes' the phenomenon sans a localized observer.

Eventually, only awareness itself prevails, and all is spontaneous and nondual. The mind is bypassed and surrendered to Mind, which is autonomous. With practice, the capacity to be 'at one' with the silent, thoughtless state can be maintained with the eyes open. One then lives within the silent state.

In the beginning, the state is lost when it is necessary to return to functioning or necessary mentation. With practice, however, even that distraction can be transcended, and the silent state prevails even though the persona goes about relating and acting in the world.

Eventually, the inner state prevails and selfless action operates spontaneously and autonomously. It is the karmic 'wind-up toy'. It can eventually even think and respond to the world without interrupting the state of silent peace.

The persona is perceived by the world to be 'you', whereas it is only a linear functionality. It is like the ripples or waves of the ocean. As with contemplation, the sense of Self moves from content to context. One then abides in the silent awareness that Ramana Maharshi termed *turiya*, or the "fourth state."

Q: Does that not result in impairment of functioning?

A: Yes. It may be necessary to leave the ordinary world for some years. At that point, it is of no concern. The world is surrendered to God.

Q: What replaces the mind when it disappears?

A: Divine wisdom unfolds. Consciousness/awareness remains but it is an autonomous quality or condition. Loss of mind does not result in 'nothingness'; on the contrary, it is replaced by Allness. The leaf is not the tree. It is safe to abandon any identification with what one thinks or believes one is for none of it is real, and 'nothingness' is purely an imagination.

Q: But what of existence itself?

A: Both existence and nonexistence are abstract positionalities. Neither term applies to Reality, which is beyond both ideas. Consciousness is as the primordial clear Light of Awareness. It is the primary condition.

Q: But wouldn't that take one to the Void?

A: That is a subject to be specifically addressed later. It is not a problem in the beginning and only becomes an issue that needs to be clarified and understood at consciousness level 850. However, it is important to know about it considerably well in advance; therefore, it is addressed at depth in a later section (see Chapter 8).

Contemplation

Meditation and contemplation are merely descriptive styles. They are not separate because the processes are essentially the same. In practice, traditional formal meditation is a process that requires removal from the activities of daily life. However, it tends to develop a certain specialness and becomes compartmentalized and sporadic over time. There are periods of enthusiasm, but the practice is vulnerable to the demands of daily life. It is more profitable to apply the essential mudra/position/focus/intention in a style that can be done continuously so that contemplation becomes a lifestyle, with one's life becoming the meditation. The evolution is to turn one's life into a prayer/contemplation/meditation/supplication and surrender. One's life becomes the prayer—the prayer is the contemplation.

The contemplative lifestyle facilitates transfer of the sense of identity from body/mind to witness/observer, which is more primary and closer to the Truth of the Self and Reality. The next step is the withdrawal of the sense of 'I' from the witness/observer, where it moves to the faculty of consciousness/awareness itself, which is a quality rather than a personage. One major advantage of being the witness/observer instead of the participant is that the witness does not talk; it just sees without comment. It could be said that the witness/observer is aligned with the forest rather than the trees.

Q: How can contemplation be instituted, started, or learned? It is a decision?

A: It is only a matter of awareness. It is really nothing new and therefore does not need to be learned but only given attention. A useful decision or choice is to decide to stop mentally talking about everything and refrain from interjecting comments, opinions, preferences, and value statements. It is therefore a discipline to just watch without evaluating, investing worth in, or editorializing, commenting, and having preferences about what is witnessed. One then sees the rising and falling away of phenomena and the transitory nature of appearance, which, with ordinary mentation, is conceptualized as a sequence of cause and effect. It is an informative practice to 'pretend' to be stupid, and by the invocation of radical humility, Essence shines forth. All thinking, from a spiritual viewpoint, is merely vanity, illusion, and pomposity. The less one thinks, the more delightful life becomes. Thinkingness eventually becomes replaced by knowingness. That one 'is' does not really need any thought at all. It is helpful, therefore, to make a decision to stop mental conversation and useless babbling.

Silent group retreats are often valuable experiences for it is discovered that life goes right on in a delightful fashion, and everything falls into place of its own accord. Communication continues nonverbally, and everyone just seems to become telepathic in a surprisingly short time.

Q: Is a contemplative lifestyle possible in today's world?

A: With strong intention, daily life conforms. Contemplation implies nonattachment, which does not preclude activity.

Q: Contemplation seems to be confrontive to the mind's propensity to control and think that it has to control in order to survive.

A: That is so. By practice, there is the emergence of the awareness that all takes place spontaneously as a consequence of the overall field plus intention, and 'you' as the imaginary causal agent were never necessary in the first place.

Q: But is not control necessary to survival?

A: Let God worry about your survival. If it serves the Self to dump the body, so let it be. In a strict spiritual practice, the time will come when one actually has permission to leave the worldly body. One witnesses whether the body will continue to walk on and breathe again or not. In the end, what one conceives to be oneself has to be surrendered to God. If it serves Providence, this bodily life continues, and if it does not, then it ceases. The eventuality is up to the Presence.

Q: It sounds as though serious spiritual work may eventually preclude one's customary lifestyle.

A: That is so. Some devotees actually leave, some become renunciates, and others modify their lifestyle to be in accord with their serious spiritual commitment. The challenge brings up issues to be processed, such as attachments to others, to possessions, to lifestyle, and to concepts such as duty, obligation, responsibility, etc. In the end, to the true devotee, the pursuit of spiritual reality supersedes all other considerations. The commitment to become enlightened involves the decision "No matter what."

Q: That sounds alarming.

A: The entity who is alarmed and seems confronted by such a situation is not the same one who asks the question. The need for a critical major decision does not arise until sufficient strength is present to handle it. That is why it is unwise to try to force spiritual progress by artificial means. To facilitate it is one thing; to try to force it is another.

CHAPTER 5

Clarifications

Paradoxically, the way of nonduality is the 'doing' of undoing. There is nonreliance on scripture or external authority. Truth stands revealed on its own without proclamation or need of aggrandizement. Its Absolute Sovereignty shines forth without need of acclaim or praise. It is, therefore, the way of faith and trust which relies on the truth that both the destination, as has been known throughout the centuries, and the means or method of discovering that truth are reliable and certain.

Traditionally, reliance has been placed on reputation or hearsay, along with historical documentation. The reliability of information was also a matter of faith and belief. In contrast, there is now a method of discerning truth from falsehood that is independent of history, ecclesiastical agreement, or reputation. It is therefore possible to quickly and easily verify not only truth from falsehood, but also to ascertain the level of that truth. That was the purpose of the research reported in *Truth vs. Falsehood.*

Whereas previous eras in the evolution of human society were characterized by faith in authority, the current era is one of doubt, challenge, and skepticism. Current society is stressed by vociferous contention, like an endless court drama of conflicting opinions and repetitious exaggeration of contradictory evidence. The purpose is to enlist support for positionalities via persuasion. It is an era of inexorably ostentatious disputation and rhetorical bombast that glorifies narcissism by subverting and distorting truth.

Historically, contention arose in the evolution of religions, and religious strife continues in the world of today, just as it has for many past centuries. Inasmuch as opinions are subjective, biased, and often consist primarily of hearsay, they cannot be depended on when it comes to crucial matters.

While worldly concerns are indeed important when the lives of millions of people depend on them, from the highest view, they are of secondary importance to spiritual truth, the consequences of which are very long term in contrast to transitory worldly life. Therefore, to trust one's spiritual evolution to some authoritative source of information is a major step that should not be taken lightly. The downside of religious/spiritual fallacy is as calamitous as that of trusting corporeal life to the nonintegrous. Therefore, before embarking on a quest, a student should verify whether a specified pathway meets critical criteria. There are many false and seriously limited spiritual/religious belief systems, teachers, and organizations. It is well to remember that the perceptions of the ego/mind are limited and subject to the seductions of illusion and impressionability. The mind itself is unable to discern truth from falsehood or to discern Descartes' *res interna* (cogitans) from *res extensa/externa* (Reality-Creation as it is).

The first requirement of spiritual integrity is to verify a pathway by all means possible, which include:

1. Historic record.
2. The effects of the alleged truths upon the world. ("By their fruits ye shall know them.")
3. Concordance with calibrated levels of consciousness.
4. Verification by subjective experiential realization.

Spiritual Education

Fortunate is the seeker who has not been led away from the straight and narrow path by diversions and popularized attractions. People spend lifetimes searching for authentic teachings and become sidetracked by the seduction of attractive, glamorized aberrations from truth. These turn out to be fictional or romanticized fantasies that attract the naïve person's inner child. Spiritual fairy tales abound and impress the credulous for whom anything labeled 'spiritual' is imbued with a magical glamour. To go through that stage is routine during initial, uncritical enthusiasm and exploration.

The primary problem initially is the lack of awareness of the difference between the truly spiritual reality and the astral, paranormal, or supernatural domains. To the naïve, these latter alternatives seem amazing and impressive. This is due to the discovery that there are surprisingly more areas for human experience than the strictly physical, emotional, and mental ones. Consequently, a 'right-on' psychic reading is indeed impressive to an erstwhile, naïve seeker or novitiate. It is also easy to become sidetracked by the seemingly astonishing wonder of a whole new dimension of possible realities.

The majority of popular best-selling, supposedly spiritual books is actually fictional, and their average level of truth is at calibration level 190, as are slick-appearing 'spiritual' magazines that glamorize fallacious fantasies of 'other dimensions', and so on. The paradox is that the appeal is to the naïve seeker who has not yet mastered *this dimension*, much less other fanciful ones.

There are, of course, other dimensions and ultimate realities that are well represented by adepts, trance readers, channelers, psychics, clairvoyants, shamans, magicians, 'masters', deceased celebrities, erstwhile guides, 'teachers', guides, fortune tellers, card readers, astrologers, throwers of Rune stones, and more. To add to the glamour, many of these diversions have large collections of faithful followers and enthusiasts who are impressed and thereby influenced, as well as seduced, by the magical notion of the unseen paranormal. Also popular are 'ancient secret mysteries', UFO religions, primitive rites, magic symbols, crystals, incantations, energy manipulation, and spirits from other realms.

Classical spiritual tradition and integrous scripture do not refute the supernatural/paranormal, but warn 'not to go there'. The same advice is also prescribed by all true spiritual masters and enlightened teachers. By consciousness calibration research, all such 'entities' on the 'other side' can be calibrated, as well as 'fallen gurus' from other eras who succumbed to the illusory gain of power over others by spiritual seduction. (See Lewis, 2001; Partridge, 2003.)

The so-called 'astral circus' was at its most influential in ancient Mesopotamia. The expertise of the adepts, many of whom are still the same as they were in that era, have perfected their skills over long periods of earthly time. Like an experienced expert salesman, they intuitively pick up on a vulnerability or a weakness, especially the proneness to glamorization. If such entities were indeed what they claim to be, they would have long ago evolved on to the celestial realms.

There is no lack of integrous, reliable spiritual truth accessible by ordinary means. Thus, the seeking of the extraordinary is a trap for the unwary. An ego that is 'out of body' is actually just the same as an ego in a body, except that it now has the mystification of being physically elusive. Exploration of other dimensions can be facilitated and learned by induced and altered states of consciousness. The primary temptation is one of child-like curiosity. On the other hand, there are some entities on the 'other side' that calibrate over 200 but they do not have any information that is not available by ordinary means (e.g., be kind to your neighbor).

Supranormal qualities arise as an experiential reality when consciousness levels reach the high 500s as a consequence of the rising *kundalini* spiritual energy field. These phenomena, classically termed *siddhis*, are the normal expression of consciousness levels that are beyond the linear. The student is advised to be aware that they are not personal and to merely witness the phenomena. By so doing, it will be evident that the phenomena are qualities specific to the spiritual energy itself; they are not personal because they are not controllable by the person. The phenomena, on the other hand, can be impressive as one witnesses the seemingly miraculous events unfold effortlessly. The reason they appear to be miraculous is because of their being witnessed by the linear mind with its limited perception of cause and effect. The unfolding of the seeming miraculous is merely 'normal' from a higher perspective.

These paranormal spiritual phenomena are described by mystics and saints of various religious denominations and have been reported throughout the ages. By calibration, 'sainthood' represents level 570 and above. The siddhis are indeed somewhat wondrous to behold, and the spiritual energy field may, of its own, transmit to other people so that healings take place in accord with karmic propensities. The 'miraculous' is thus not volitional or controllable, nor is it the consequence of any person; thus, there is no 'person' who performs miracles. It is instead the consequence of the healing power of the Self.

The siddhis arise of their own and bring about the capacity for psychometry, clairvoyance, clairaudience, distant vision, and other telepathic types of faculties. They are also unpredictable and evanescent. Some come and go over variable periods of time that may last from weeks to months to a number of years. With forewarning, the student who witnesses and experiences these phenomena can easily dismiss the temptation of ownership and its implied specialness. Integrity and humility preclude claiming authorship of the phenomena and thus being trapped by an illusion. The siddhis are discussed at some length in *Transcending the Levels of Consciousness*.

From a practical viewpoint, the appearance of the siddhis is also a signal to begin making arrangements about worldly affairs as performing some of them may be coming to an end. It is a matter of wisdom to make 'practical' decisions while it is still possible to do so. Capacities may change, as well as motivations and values, and what previously seemed to be of great value and worth may later appear as a waste of time and effort. Thus, such things as success and opulence become amusements, and finally nuisances and then distractions. This shift of viewpoints is consequent to the evolution of consciousness, which has moved from want/have/seek to effortless attraction by virtue of what one has become.

At the lower levels of consciousness, effort is

applied within the context of cause and effect, but as evolution of consciousness progresses, phenomena are the consequence of attraction by the energy field itself rather than as a consequence of personal volition. At a higher level, it is only necessary to 'be with' rather than to 'own'.

The spiritual information necessary for advanced states should be learned early and stored away for when it is needed. The possible downside of hearing advanced information early is the intellect's presumption of prideful 'I know that'. It is better to hold the information as 'I have heard that'. To truly 'know' is to 'be', at which point one does not know; instead, one 'is'.

The dedication to Self-realization and Enlightenment is a disciplined straight-and-narrow path. Thus, a serious devotee is advised to bypass the attraction of curiosity and appeal to the inner child of the magical and mysterious paranormal and psychic phenomena that are commonly merchandised and proffered as learnable skills. These are delays and also traps for the unwary. Their appeal is to the exotic, foreign, occult, and esoteric elaborations that are intriguing but do not lead to Enlightenment. Most are merely imitations of the genuine phenomena and lead to involvement in linear interests and manipulations of energies.

Mystical 'powers' that are genuine are not exhibited, much less promoted or sold for a price. Imitations of the real are a diversion that have sidetracked and deceived many naïve spiritual students and even branches of major religions (Tibetan Tantric yogas, pseudolevitation, Tantric sex, etc.) Artificial means are ego inflating as is denoted by the mere fact that one is attracted to them by their specialness and the glamour of the unique and unusual. Even when acquired by training, such phenomena are merely acquired skills that have been sought for their own sake and reflect spiritual vanity as evidenced by display and promotion.

While the gifts of God can be imitated, the forgery is not the genuine. This can be ascertained by consciousness level calibration. The genuine siddhis start to emerge at calibration level 540 and become predominant in the range of level 570. The promoted imitations calibrate from 155 to the lower 400s. Notable also is that no Avatars or great Teachers recommend the seeking of the supernatural.

Miraculous phenomena are the spontaneous, non-volitional emergence of a potentiality's emerging as an actuality as a consequence of karmic propensities and local conditions, such as the level of the contextual field set by the power of the prevailing level of consciousness.

Mixing Levels

In addition to the ego/mind's presumption that it 'knows' something because it has heard about it (reading a book on golf does not make one an expert golfer), there is the error of mixing levels of truth or abstraction. The apparent realities of a specific level of consciousness are not necessarily those of another level, as is indicated by the numerical designations of the calibrated levels of consciousness. As an example, one can cite the well-known saying of Ramana Maharshi that "there is no point in trying to save the world because the world one sees does not even exist." That is the truth and experiential reality of consciousness calibration level 720, but it is not the experiential reality of consciousness levels below it. It is necessary to be true to the reality that is experientially valid and true at one's level of development.

Each level also has its concordant capacities as well as its limitations, which are quite different. For example, perhaps Ramana Maharshi could safely walk across a busy highway with his eyes shut, but that is unlikely to be the experience of the average person who is probably not able to imitate the same behavior without getting run over.

The error of mixing levels explains why there were people who took LSD and then jumped out the window because they believed that they were bodiless and could fly. The rules of out-of-body states are decidedly different from in-the-body states. Comparably, one could make the mistake of assuming that because the ego/mind operates on an illusory basis, one is therefore not karmically answerable for decisions, deeds, and actions. Each person is responsible at their own level of consciousness and not at some other hypothetical ideal. The error can be understood by realizing that the truth is the consequence of not only content but also of context. Thus, karmically, everyone is accountable and culpable within the reality of their own level of consciousness at a given time.

Mixing levels of abstraction is also a defect of reason in the intellectual domain (e.g. relativism), where ignoring context results in absurdities, for what is truth at one level of abstraction is false at another. This accounts for the well-known fallacies of rhetoric that ignore either context or the rules of logic, or both.

Each level of consciousness influences perceived

significance, understanding, and meaning, and thus, accountability is concordant with comprehension. This is also a principle even in law, for to know or not to know certain facts is important to the judge and the jury. Thus, culpability is a variable dependent on circumstances, conditions, and such factors as age, mental condition, motives, etc. It is true that the 'who' you are now is not the same as the 'who' you will be at a later level of evolution. Each 'who' has a different level of culpability.

Constancy

Effective spiritual endeavor is a consequence of constancy and persistence rather than fits and starts of enthusiasm. Each state of spiritual evolution is self-rewarding, gratifying, and complete unto itself. The moments of prior anguish are found to have been worth the effort.

In addition to inner-directed spiritual effort, the 'karma yoga' of selfless service is also supportive of the evolution of consciousness. Inner satisfaction becomes more important than worldly gain or the desire to control or influence others. Attraction replaces promotion. Eventually, resistances are no longer related to worldly life and its perceived values. Instead, the inner intention is one of purity and selflessness. Thus, evolution becomes the consequence of the process itself rather than as a consequence of seekingness or acquisition.

With spiritual evolution, nurturance is no longer sought from the narcissistic ego but instead from the Self. Fulfillment of potential is rewarding in and of itself and is not needful of recognition or gain. Pleasure at gain is replaced by gratitude for the unfolding of the inner process itself. The need for externals disappears spontaneously. The evolutionary process requires less and less effort as it becomes a way of being in the world. Transition and transformation are self-actuating as a response of the Self to entreaty by the self. The pace of spiritual evolution is not under personal control and may take sudden, surprising leaps. Therefore, it is wise to prepare beforehand with knowledge of what yet may come.

It is important to realize that the destiny of those who choose Enlightenment is Enlightenment—who else would be on such a quest? To merely seek spiritual purification and awareness is already a great gift. There is no point to wondering, How am I doing? for the compass has already been set by dedication and devotion to the highest truth. While the pace may seem slow or even arduous at times, it is best to be prepared for sudden, unexpected leaps. It is wise to avoid pessimism, even after a seemingly long, dry period of frustration, for such periods are due to overcoming major obstacles and attachments that often presage major changes.

An unseen benefit of spiritual endeavor and evolution is its positive influence on the collective level of human consciousness itself. Each evolving spiritual devotee counterbalances the negative effect of great numbers of people of a considerably lower consciousness level. Consciousness calibration research reveals that the collective consciousness level of mankind is moving upward. Thus, an optimistic view is warranted. One can be grateful to have been born a human with all its infinite potential for karmic benefit. One can also be grateful that they have heard of Enlightenment and have chosen to seek it, for such individuals are extremely rare indeed. As reported in prior works, statistically, the likelihood of a person's choosing Enlightenment as the major purpose of one's life is one in ten million persons.

Q: To choose to pursue Enlightenment is uncommon in our current society, with its emphasis on worldliness and the dominance of the media that in turn focus on the contentious or glamorize the superficial. What true value can be derived from worldly life?

A: The world can be seen as an optimal stimulus for inner growth as it is merely a projection of the ego in overt dramatic expression. It is best to learn from it rather than to be seduced by its illusions or entrapped by them via identification or attachment. The worldly panorama reflects the entire scale of the levels of consciousness in their most overt display. The panorama is like a school of discernment where the extremes serve to reveal the essence that underlies appearance.

Q: How can one simultaneously participate yet not get attached or involved? Does that not lead to avoidance?

A: It is the motive that determines the effects of participation. Activities are merely what one 'does', but not what one 'is'. All seeming events present learning opportunities. One can participate and at the same time experience phenomena from the level of the witness/observer and watch what arises from within the psyche. It is important to differentiate detachment from nonattachment. Detachment can result in avoidance or withdrawal, whereas nonattachment allows for participation without taking a stake in the outcome.

Q: How then should one best relate to the world?
A: To be 'in' it but not 'of' it. The world is a means and not an end. Nonattached interaction reveals habitual styles and attitudes that are consequent to inner ego positionalities. It is interesting and educative to note how others relate to the same circumstances. One can experiment with different personality styles and, with flexibility, discover untapped inner resources. This is the classic 'as if' experiment.

One often avoids situations based on presumptions and their subsequent resistances. An instructive practice is to pretend either in imagination or in daily life to enjoy certain activities and people and then surprisingly discover that the capacity for enjoyment and pleasure stems from within (i.e., *joie de vivre*). Experimenting with other attitudes and personality styles results in surprising inner discoveries. This type of 'role playing' is utilized in the group techniques of psychodrama.

Q: How can one really discern what is important from that which is superficial and evanescent?
A: Intention services techniques and learning styles. A simple one is to mentally view one's life as though it were on 'fast forward' on a recording/playback machine. One then sees the body rapidly moving through multiple activities, relationships, overt behaviors, and progressive age periods. Eventually the 'fast forward' moves to the end of the physicality,

which is confrontive and brings out evaluation of the importance of life goals, projected values, and significance, such as the fulfillment of potential. When the tape comes to the end of life, the questions automatically arise: What has been done of value? For what would one wish to be accountable? One can imagine different viewpoints and see the different choices and options that would have been made.

Q: The attractions of the world seem endless. Is it really safe to go there? I often just want to escape.

A: The attractions are not innate to the world but reflect projected values and the expectation of the payoffs of ego satisfactions. In actuality, joy stems from within and is not dependent on externals. Pleasure is associated with what is valued and esteemed. Much of projected value arises from imagination, and values reflect desires. In reality, nothing is more valuable than anything else other than spiritual fulfillment. Routinely, people discover that the life of a celebrity is onerous and burdensome once the novelty has worn off. Imagined pleasures are really of the senses and the emotions. With inner spiritual evolution, all activities become equal.

Q: What about action?

A: Actions are the automatic consequence of the integration of context, field, and intention. All action is actually spontaneous and reflects karmic propensities and local conditions that may or may not favor expression. To depersonalize actions, it is only necessary to let go of the belief that there is a separate, independent causal agent called 'I' or 'me'. This awareness allows for the development of the 'non-action of action', which is possible by relinquishment of trying to control results. The only thing one can actually 'do' is to 'be' one's potential to the fullest. That 'one is responsible for the effort but not the result' is a twelve–step program basic dictum that curbs the ego.

Existence is its own reward. It is more gratifying in the long term to fulfill potentiality than to try to achieve results. Therefore, one becomes aligned with excellence of performance for its own sake.

Everything in existence is already 'being' what it is to the fullest it can be at any given moment. The 'non-action' of action does not move from imperfection to perfection, or from incomplete to complete, but instead from complete to complete and from perfection to perfection. All is perfect by virtue of its identity's being exactly its meaning, which is its existence. The perfect seed transforms and metamorphoses via emergence into being the perfect sprout, and then as the perfect bud, then the perfect flower, and then the perfect faded flower. All form is perfectly just what it is at any given moment. Creation moves from perfectly 'this' to perfectly 'that'. There is no other possibility except in the imagination. Everything already is exactly as it is 'supposed' to be. A nice, old, dilapidated, dented trashcan is 'supposed' to look beat up or it would not be a nice, old, beat-up trashcan. (The ego wants a shiny new one, of course.)

Q: Is 'time' itself an illusion?

A: Creation manifests as emergence, which, to the perception of the ego, is interpreted as 'change'. What is witnessed is potentiality's manifesting as actuality, which becomes contextualized as 'becoming'. The ego superimposes a time track, which is a projection. There is only continuous awareness. Time is a mental construct and an attempt to conceptualize an explanation for sequence. Sequence is itself a conceptualization of the observer and a mentation. The actual Reality is not comprehensible to the mind.

As the ego collapses, time vanishes and all phenomena appear to be in slow motion. This truth was uncannily intuited by a few cinematographers, such as appears in the slow-motion scenes in the movie *Deep Blue* (cal. 700) and the movie of the life of St. Francis of Assisi, *Francis of Assisi*. The Reality is subjective, experiential, and revelatory rather than conceptual.

Investigation of even the seemingly trivial reveals that perceptual linear duality is a product of the imagination, which in turn is based on the fallacy of the hypothetical. Everything at every second is already the perfect expression of its karmic potentiality based on prevailing conditions that influence the emergence of potentiality's becoming actuality. Everything is the presentation of that which it is, for everything already is exactly what it is, which again is its meaning, its worth, and its value. 'Worth' and 'value' are projected mentalizations. A crooked tree is a perfect crooked tree. If it were not a perfect crooked tree, it would be a perfect straight tree. There is no basic difference.

Q: **Nonduality is like a radical reality in which everything is seen as the expression of its essence by virtue of its identity.**

A: That is an essential insight. All Creation, in and of itself, moves from perfection to perfection solely by virtue of its existence. Existence is already the fulfillment of potentiality expressed as the actuality.

Form is a consequence of local conditions and is again the perfect expression possible under prevailing conditions. All objections or doubts about the perfection of Creation stem from *res interna/cogitans*, which projects the hypothetical error onto the world.

In contrast, via the Heisenberg principle in quantum mechanics, the details of the evolutionary change can be contextualized in mathematical formulas. Intention (consciousness) collapses the wave function from the potential to the actual, from the potential state of the universe (the Schrödinger equations) to the collapsed wave state (the Dirac equation). The new state then becomes the new potential state that then 'collapses' into the next defined state.

The state of Enlightenment is therefore the potential Reality that replaces the illusions of the ego's perceptual positionalities. Spiritual intention, effort, and decision potentiate the evolution of consciousness from the linear limited to the nonlinear Allness of Reality. Thus again, intention activates the progress from possibility to probability to actuality.

Q: **In the lectures, you mentioned the example of Roger Bannister's breaking the belief system of the four-minute mile. How does that relate to spiritual work?**

A: Each individual who transcends the levels of con-sciousness to their highest completion in this domain makes it easier for others to follow, just like the lead dog breaks the snow and facilitates the progress of the rest of the team. One's seeming individual spiritual endeavor serves all mankind. Each one who crosses over from below 200 to above 200 has already enabled untold numbers to follow and serves as a potential instructor as well. One cannot become enlightened just for one's own self because the impact is felt throughout all of human consciousness.

The spiritual seeker of today has the advantage that the consciousness level of all mankind is rising, and thus, there is less collective resistance.

CHAPTER 6

The "Experiencer"

The mind acts as a processor of data simultaneously from both within and without. It categorizes, sorts, prioritizes, contextualizes, and interprets simultaneously as it concordantly draws on memory banks, emotional centers, and conditioned responses and their correlations. All the above are orchestrated contextually with emotional/animal instincts that are sorted, rejected, accepted, or modified. In addition, this multilayered complexity is simultaneously subject to options, choices, and the will. Options and choices related to meaning and value overall are under the influence and dominance of an all-inclusive, overall field of consciousness having concordant and variable levels of power related to the level of consciousness that is also influenced by karmic propensities. Simultaneously, the mind assesses degrees of relative truth, credibility of information, and suitability and probabilities of action within similarly multilayered behavioral social limits, including moral, ethical, social, and religious principles.

This complex, integrated processing system amazingly operates within approximately 1/10,000th of a second, during which it simultaneously selects and processes thoughts, ideas, and images that are invested with emotion and categorized estimates of importance. The mind is therefore like an infinitely complex processing unit of both internal and external data. Some of the information is perceived and stored in memory banks, but there is also unconscious processing of all the data that is stored in the unconscious. This processing screening device results in the 1/10,000th of a second's delay and acts as a separation between self and Self/Reality. This processing screen represents 'the experiencer' in action.

Transcending the Experiencer

Between phenomena and the experience of the phenomena is the 1/10,000th of a second's delay; thus, the output is like the tape monitor playback of a tape recorder that processes information during that split second between reception and reproduction. The important point is to realize that the self receives only processed material and not the original. In addition, the processed material then interacts with the automated response of the personal self to the edited data.

Although the ego/mind processor performs an incredibly complex multitude of functions simultaneously and seemingly without effort, there is a loss between input and output. That loss is a quality of the original purity and innate brilliance. The output to the 'experiencer' is devoid of the aliveness and radiance of Divinity that is innate to All that Exists. With the evolution of consciousness, this screen suddenly disappears, and when this happens, there is a profound transformation in that everything becomes radiant, illuminated in depth, texture, and color. It 'presents' itself unedited instead of being perceived and interpreted.

The experiencer screen is energized by desire and identification with it. This desire is like an appetite of curiosity, wantingness, and craving, and is an addiction to the experience of experiencing itself. In addition, there is identification with experiencing and its content information as 'self'. Thus the mind says, 'I' saw, heard, felt, thought, etc. This would therefore seem to be rather a natural misidentification as the experiencer is the leading edge of perception and sensation. Misidentification arose during the evolution of consciousness to subserve survival needs.

From its earliest appearance in evolution, animal life forms were inherently defective in that they lacked an intrinsic source of energy. Therefore, energy had to be sought and detected for assimilation. The basic essential core program of the primitive ego was to sample, explore, forage, seek, and 'get'. Thus, from its earliest onset, animal life was innately lacking the means to survival and therefore had to constantly search to find and identify the energy sources and substances that then needed to be assimilated and absorbed from its environment. This necessitated the development of information detection, gathering, and integration systems to evaluate the input (edible versus inedible, friend versus enemy, etc.). The result was the evolution of a primordial ego-survival system to process, identify, compare, and categorize priorities of survival information that heralded the onset of learning and intelligence. This experiencer process became the 'I' of separate identity. Although it became greatly diversified and elaborated over the millennia, its core identification and function remained essentially the same.

The overall intention, motivation, and alignment of this core ego process to survive by getting and controlling dominates the consciousness levels below 200, which are characterized by the term 'egocentricity', indicating aggressive self-interest and the predominance of the animal-like predatory qualities. This may be seen in an undisguised style in the psychopath where these characteristics are acted out pathologically, as well as through gross demonstration by narcissistic

messianic leaders who represent the primitive limitation of consciousness development. At consciousness
level 200, there is the emergence of awareness and the
recognition of the equal value and worth of others, sig-
nifying the appearance of spiritual energy that transforms context, paradigm, and intention.

The interface of the processor/experiencer is the
core of separation and duality. It is also the focus of
identity, and the separate 'I' sees the self, therefore, as
the source of life and existence. The core of spiritual
work is to undo this ancient programming. The self
identifies not only with the mind/experiencer but also
with its content, which becomes 'my' memory, 'my'
senses, 'my' thoughts, 'my' emotions, 'my' property, 'my'
success, 'my' failure, 'my' expectations, 'my' feelings, and
so on. Identification presumes ownership and authorship; thus, the ego sees and believes itself to be a personal, separate causal agent and the inferred source of
its own existence. The self projects the duality onto
the world where phenomena are conceptualized in
terms of cause and effect. Inasmuch as the self is presumed to be a causal agent, it is therefore also the
object of guilt, pride, fear, and all the emotions. The
self becomes equated with being the source of life
and thus having the qualities of Divinity. The
ego/mind subtly worships the self and treats it as
though it were Divine.

The inflated ego, such as is shown by the narcissistic
personality, demonstrates overtly the famous 'king
baby' attitude that is the core of the human ego. It
surfaces in society as the narcissistic personality that
expects its whims, wishes, and inflated self-importance
to be catered to. It characteristically feels 'entitled',

'made uncomfortable', 'sensitive', and the victim of perceived 'slights' and injustices and seeks redress by protest, drama, and hand-wringing self-pity.

In deprogramming the experiencer from the evolutionary development of the ego with its multifunction complexity, it can be seen why spiritual evolution takes time plus effort, awareness, and high motivation. To undo this complex mind/ego/experiencer/self apparatus sequentially is not possible without the motivation or assistance of a specific spiritual energy that has the necessary power. Traditionally, this spiritual energy was labeled kundalini to indicate its serpentine course as it rises up the energy channels of the spine through the ascending energy centers, traditionally termed 'chakras'. This unique, transformative energy, which appears at consciousness level 200, changes the physiology and dynamics of the brain, including hemispheric dominance. Consequently, there is a shift in brain hormones and neurotransmitters (see following chart).

BRAIN FUNCTION AND PHYSIOLOGY

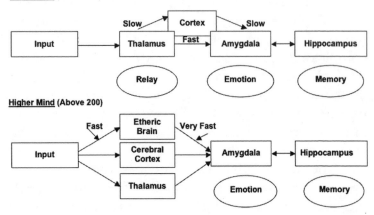

Below 200	Above 200
Left-brain dominance	Right-brain dominance
Linear	Non-linear
Stress – Adrenaline	Peace – Endorphins
Fight or flight	Positive emotion
Alarm – Resistance – Exhaustion (Selye – Cannon: Fight/Flight)	Support thymus
▼ Killer cells and immunity	▲ Killer cells
Thymus stress	▲ Immunity
Disrupt acupuncture meridian	Healing
Disease	Balanced acupuncture system
Negative kinesiological response	Positive kinesiological response
▼ Neurotransmitters – Serotonin	
Track to emotions twice as fast as through prefrontal cortex to emotions	Track to emotion slower than from prefrontal and etheric cortexes

Importance:
Spiritual endeavor and intention change the brain function and the body's physiology and establish a specific area for spiritual information in the right-brain prefrontal cortex and its concordant etheric (energy) brain.

Of interest is that the altered brain chemistry is also influenced by facilitating mechanisms that are activated by experience. Certain genes become expressive only as a result of stress, and others activate only under favorable experiences, thus demonstrating the influence of both nature and nurture. A positive shift in brain physiology is also favored by positive early-life experiences, such as exposure to classical music, beauty, esthetics, and religious upbringing, which further activate genetic propensities and neuronal patterning. (As mentioned in earlier works, these favorable, early-life experiences reduce criminality by approximately ninety percent.)

The problem with the processor/experiencer ego is not just its composition but also its dominance, which only becomes diminished by the influx of spiritual energy. With the onset of the kundalini spiritual energy, there is, for the first time in evolution, the development of an etheric brain consisting solely of energy. This spiritual-energy etheric brain identifies with context rather than content, whereas the animal-ego/narcissistic-processor self relates to content. Animal-brain processing sees things in terms of cause and effect and sees self as causal. The spiritual etheric brain sees self as a participant and is capable of seeing phenomena as the activation of potentiality. The spiritual energy's effect is the capacity to comprehend nondualistically and thus to eventually develop the capacity to discern essence from appearance.

Q: The spiritual seeker of today is advantaged by having information that was not available in the past. On the other hand, there seems to be more data to assimilate. Is it necessary to comprehend all of it?

A: No, it is supplied primarily for the sake of utility to facilitate success on the journey that historically has been described as quite difficult. With the addition of new information and the advancement of consciousness overall, the likelihood of reaching advanced states of consciousness is one thousand percent greater than before. To even decide on such a mission is already a sign of major spiritual evolution.

The purpose of supplying a great deal of supportive data is to provide the means of corroborating the truth of the information. Thus, it provides a bulwark against misinterpretation, which historically has frequently been the fate of spiritual truth.

Q: Why is truth itself, and especially spiritual truth, so subject to distortion and misinterpretation?

A: The ego's survival relies on the defeat of truth because it is dependent on allegiance to falsity and illusion. For one thing, spiritual truth challenges the ego's presumption that it is sovereign. This is seen socially in the rising popularity of secularism, which seeks to eliminate all references to Divinity or spiritual truth, or even the basics of morality or ethics. The current appeal of relativism (cal. 180-190) is that it subserves the ego's wish to reign supreme by virtue of the statement that there is no absolute truth at all. This currently promoted philosophy is actually based on nihilism (cal. 50) and is the rationale for the social promotion of nonintegrity by political distortion. Truth therefore has opponents from both within and outside religion.

Q: The total content of the mind, including its memory, is vast and includes multimillions of bits of information as well as a dazzling multitude of complex operational functions. The task of overcoming its dominance seems overwhelming and even intimidating.

A: It does indeed seem like a Herculean task when viewed from a linear perspective; however, the foundations of its content and operations are similar to a computer's motherboard that, when disconnected, unplugs entire, sizeable sets of operations. One could also say that, analogously, each level of consciousness is orchestrated by its own predominant energy attractor field (see "nonlinear dynamics" in *Power vs. Force,* [Hawkins, 1995]), which is thereby the operational 'motherboard' for that field.

To choose to forgive by giving up the 'juice' of justified resentments and grudges disconnects all the associated thoughts and grievances from them, along with their multiple rationalizations and memories. Thus, each level has its basic props, and when these props are surrendered, the level no longer dominates. By removing the motherboards of each level, one witnesses that everything merely is just what it is, and judgmentalism is surrendered to God.

Each level has its associated negative feelings, including guilt, shame, fear, etc., so removing its fulcrum allows the whole stack to collapse. Each step along the way is self-rewarding and reinforces dedication to the process. With removal of the positionality that results in a whole level of consciousness, the negative energy disappears and is replaced by the positive spiritual energies. As the process proceeds, there is therefore less and less resistance.

Q: What is the most useful information to know? Is there a major key understanding?

A: Resistance subsides when there is a clear understanding that what is being surrendered is not of intrinsic value but is instead imagined to be of value solely because of the juice or payoff the ego extracts from that position. The principle of willingness need only be applied to the ego's payoff and not to the object or condition desired.

One can ask oneself the question, Is this worth giving up God for? Thus, ego positionality has a price, which is where the willingness should be addressed. Each positionality is based on the presumption that its fulfillment will bring happiness. Thus, nothing is really valued aside from the illusion that it will bring that about.

This reinforces the importance of keeping in mind Socrates' dictum that all men choose only what they perceive to be the good. It is just that they do not know what is the 'real' good. It becomes evident by consciousness research that happiness is associated only with a single factor—a level of consciousness.

Q: What is the critical central focus of the ego, i.e., its critical factor?

A: The ego is focused on one point, the experiencer, which is programmed to seek pleasure and survival through gain. It views happiness as something one acquires, possesses, and incorporates. Therefore, the experiencer is programmed to 'get'. The experiencer's function is to get pleasure and possess it. It is not concerned with the soul unless it fortuitously becomes spiritually oriented. Then its goals shift, and it discovers that the source of pleasure is completely within. When it is discovered that the source of ongoing pleasure is the Self, and not the self, the result is independence from the world. Gratification of the ego's desires is within the linear domain. True happiness arises from the nonlinear. With relinquishment of dependence on the experiencer for pleasure and happiness, one discovers that the source of happiness is one's own existence, and the realization of the Self is happiness itself.

Q: It seems as though the ego's attachments are multitudinous and almost overwhelming.

A: Complexity is a perception of the ego/mind. One sharp knife can cut through hundreds of different objects; there is only the necessity of one simple action. Analogously, there is only *one simple key concept* necessary to disengage from all the ego's encumbrances. It has only one addiction, which is to subjective pleasure/gain. That is the secret pay-off of *all* desires, projected values, and attractions. This is exaggerated by projected value, worth, glamour, or specialness. There is only *one* gain, and this same gain is merely superimposed on everything that is desired and therefore attracts attachment. The pleasure is associated with derived happiness. Thus, the ego has only one goal. That discernment enables escape from all attractions. This solitary motive is merely projected onto multiple diverse objects, persons, or qualities.

The clever ego can extract the juice/payoff of secret gratification and pleasure from anything it arbitrarily selects. Actually, it is always just the same goal over and over again. The 'what' that is desired is actually irrelevant. The locus is imagined to be 'out there' but is actually 'in here', for the pleasure gain is subjective and internal. The relinquishment of this single, solitary goal unveils the Reality of the Self, which is the innate prime source of all happiness, and its Realization terminates all wants and desires. The locus of happiness is always solely from within. Pleasure is transitory; joy and happiness are from within.

CHAPTER 7

The Razor's Edge

Discussion

It can be seen that even on a conceptual level, it is not possible to undo the ego/experiencer complex in a linear fashion, nor is it possible without Divine assistance, which is provided by the presence of the spiritual energy itself. The spiritual energy is an emanation of Self. The inflow of Divine energy is a consequence of karmic propensities, along with Grace, spiritual choice, and the assent of the Will as exemplified by worship, spiritual commitment, prayer, supplication, selfless service, mercy, and love.

Consciousness calibration indicates the level of the evolution of consciousness, which is correlated with the degree of dominance of the spiritual energy that accompanies truth and love. The ego cannot be undone in a serial manner through all of its multitudinous belief systems. Instead, by spiritual intention and devotion, the calibrated level moves up, and as it does, the field itself supports the undoing of the ego's dominance.

The techniques and practices that dissolve the underpinnings of the various ego positions along the Scale of Consciousness have been described elsewhere (*Transcending the Levels of Consciousness*). These have also been alluded to in the sections on meditation and contemplation. At a certain period in spiritual evolution and by assent of the will, there arises the inner decision to seriously and actively pursue spiritual awareness for its own sake. This may be accompanied by a change of lifestyle and/or the seeking out of spiritual teachers or communities. Operationally, the central elements of seriously committed inner spiritual work consist of:

1. Discipline of focus without deviation.
2. Willingness to surrender all desires and fears to God.
3. Willingness to endure transitory anguish until the difficulty is transcended.
4. Constancy and watchfulness.
5. Moving from self-interest as participant/experiencer to that of the witness/observer.
6. Willingness to relinquish judgmentalism and opinion about what is observed.
7. Identifying with the field rather than with the content of the field.
8. Proceeding with certainty and confidence by accepting that Enlightenment is one's destiny, not a goal, wish, or hope; rejecting the notion that Enlightenment is a gain; and understanding it is a condition that ensues as a consequence of decision, intention, and devotional dedication consequent to both karma and Divine Grace.
9. Avoiding glamorizing or aggrandizing the endeavor or its destination, and relying instead on devotion for its own sake.

The Razor's Edge: Staying on the Crest of the Wave

The witness/observer is a contemplative attitude of poise. Phenomena appear and disappear. One must constantly surrender the desire to experience the phenomena or the desire to 'juice' the experience of the experiencing itself.

It will be noticed that feelings and thoughts arise and fall away like waves. To anticipate the future is often the result of trying to control it based on fear. The fear, control, and anticipation are associated with focusing on the front of the wave of experiencing. In contrast, to cling to thoughts and feelings for even 1/10th of a second past the cresting wave is to focus on and cling to the past. The focus needs to be on the crest of the wave itself as it is breaking into that 1/10,000th-of-a-second aperture of 'experiencing'. The detection of this 'space' is possible by the inner quality of consciousness/awareness, which is not subject to delay. It is not possible to choose this by perception because perception moves at exactly the same rate as does mentation.

Awareness/consciousness is located just beneath or prior to the function of the watcher/observer. It is silent and unmoving, like the sky or space itself. By relinquishing anticipation, clinging, seeking pleasure, or avoiding unpleasantness, the focus remains poised on the razor's edge of the crest of the fleeting moment. By this poised position, mentation and imaging gradually recede and reveal that the underlying field is activated by the desire and intention of thinkingness itself. As focus and interest move from content to the observer/witness, it will be found that the observer/witness is an emanation of consciousness as awareness and a nonlinear, impersonal quality that is primary, innate, and autonomous.

Although this meditation/contemplation may seem unfamiliar or awkward at first, because it is in accord with the will and Divine energy, it eventually becomes self-positioning without resistance. If the witnessed data are neither desired, resisted, nor given value as 'mine', they begin to subside and eventually fall away.

In turn, each is surrendered to God as it arises, and the silent energy source that it is desirous of thinking or experiencing is revealed. To de-energize it, it is only necessary to surrender the desire to God.

Transformation/Revelation

By withdrawal of interest or value from the experiencer's filter screen of the illusory 'I'/self, the illusory self becomes an 'it' rather than an 'I'. Its dominance and interference diminish and fall away. The world's appearance and quality then demonstrate a profound change. With the removal of the interference of the processing screen, everything reveals itself as intrinsically, exquisitely radiant. Everything 'presents' itself with aliveness and awareness. The prior appearance of the world, in contrast, was drab and monochromatic compared to Technicolor. Now all shines forth its own radiance of stunning beauty consequent to the aliveness, pervasiveness, and universality of life.

All is interrelated and expressive of Oneness and Unity. All is happening spontaneously of its own. The brilliant quality of radiant beauty shines forth as the Essence of Creation. The mind becomes silent. At first hesitatingly, and then in overwhelm, it realizes that Divinity is revealing Itself like the gift of a presentation. It is uniquely Divinity's manifesting as Creation, which is continuous. All shines forth its awareness by worship and adoration of the existence of overwhelming Love as Presence. The presentation is stunning, and even the field of conscious awareness is stilled by the grandeur.

The Presence precludes functioning in the ordinary sense. The familiar self-identity has disappeared. It is not even possible to speak of the Reality without

Divine assistance. It cannot be described or explained. (To even allude to it took thirty years.)

One-Pointedness of Mind

This is a subject often brought up during lectures and is alluded to in classical spiritual literature. The basics have been described as a volitional process that is often confused with 'concentration'. It comes about instead as a consequence of focus rather than effort, which is implied by the concept of concentration. The decision is actually to 'allow' rather than to 'do'. It involves the willingness to surrender either clinging to or avoiding the parade of witnessed phenomena, whether they originate internally (mind/emotion) or externally (perception/the senses).

It is only necessary to relinquish the attraction or aversion to transitory phenomena. The term 'concentration' results in efforting as an ego focus on content, which is linear, whereas the awareness should instead withdraw from content (images, thoughts, ideas, feelings, etc.) to the nonlinear contextual field itself.

This attitude results in coming closer to the question of 'who' is watching. With inner honesty, one then discovers that there is no 'who' but instead there is a 'what', which is an autonomous quality that witnesses. It becomes detached by virtue of the withdrawal of intention to 'do' something with phenomena, such as extracting pleasure or an emotion.

A more accurate term for the process is 'nonpointedness of mind' in that it is a choice/decision to not focus and thus be drawn into participation with the passing phenomena. One merely allows the witnessing by volitional choice rather than by effortful focus of one-pointedness of concentration. The term 'one-point-edness' is specifically linear as well as dualistic in that it splits contextualization into a 'who' that is focusing on a 'what', resulting in a dualistic split between a 'this' and a 'that'. This duality subsides as a consequence of the intention to experience phenomena. Thus, it is in the opposite direction from psychological self-inquiry, which is designed to investigate how one thinks or feels while recalling life events. That type of inquiry leads to an endless quest in which each bit of information automatically leads to the next question, indicating that it is therefore a system designed to explore the ego rather than transcend it.

It will be noticed that the experiencer aspect of the ego is constantly poised to derive benefit from the witnessed phenomena, even if it is only to confirm its own reality as being the 'you' of the ever-presumptuous personal 'I'.

The ego is reluctant to accept that the unfolding of sequential phenomena is autonomous and impersonal. It is poised to jump in to impose a feeling, which in turn is always the expression of an ego viewpoint or a positionality, such as an opinion, or at least an order to declare itself to be primordially essential to one's identity and sense of reality. To cease identifying the experiencer as the reality of oneself is a major transition from dualistic content to nondualistic context, and therefore, from self to Self.

The Attraction of Phenomena

The experiencer is seduced by the lure and attraction of transitory phenomena because of projected value and worth. These are reflective of meaning, importance, and significance, which one can see is the entire basis of the industry of advertising for the purpose of gaining attention and attracting the desire to 'have', to 'do', or to 'be' (successful, admired, rich, etc.).

Thus, all witnessed phenomena are like endless solicitations to 'own', to 'claim', to 'be', and receive benefit in some magical way. The content of transitional and witnessed phenomena is therefore glamorized as having significance or value and becomes specialized, even if its only worth or meaning is that it is 'mine'. This proclivity is seen in clinical conditions where there is panic over a memory loss for an amnesic time period. This is seen in some elderly people in the early years of memory loss, but as it progresses, the majority of patients become indifferent to it and could not care less about what the date or the year are, or even how old they are. This continues to cause some panic in the nursing staff and the family but is accepted by the elderly with equanimity.

It is instructive to imagine a whole time period in one's life of which there is no memory (this has actually already happened in everyone's life but has not been noticed). At first, there is panic and the emotional melodrama of loss. Investigation of the 'what' that has been lost is quite revealing. With some reflection, the supposedly tragic loss becomes a 'so what?' Memory is given value by being sentimentalized as 'precious' because it is 'me' or 'mine'.

The experiment also reveals identification of self as a subjective, experiential, linear time track. The average adult mind is usually unable to recall the details of sizeable periods of time. Even to do so requires concentrated effort by which one is usually only able to pull up very major events. It is instructive to note that during the time period of the missing years, the ego/mind was busily experiencing and usually extracting all the imaginary payoff it could from the passing phenomena. The question to ask is, Of what value is it now?

To assist in detaching from the attractive, seductive lure of the transitory linear content of witnessed phenomena, it is helpful to imagine that what is being experienced will also likely be forgotten, usually in a matter of just a few seconds. This linear content is really not important enough to be retrieved unless it is denoted as 'special' or important. An analogy is provided by the recently discovered 'blink' phenomenon whereby the brain/mind automatically shuts off visual awareness every time the eyes blink (Bristow, 2005). As a result, in an ordinary lifetime, a total of approximately nine days is spent in visual oblivion.

Instructional exercises reveal that one is not the passive victim of mentation but instead is the very originator by virtue of intention to extract projected value. With this understanding, one is free from being dominated by the false 'I' of the experiencer.

The Self is not subject to nor limited by the experiencer. Its quality is neither linear nor sequential and is independent of phenomena and even of the practice of experiencing itself. By virtue of identity, the Self is innately simultaneously the Knower and the Known.

Q: The description of one-pointedness of mind clarifies that it is not really a special process, procedure, or demanding practice but more of a way of orientation to the transitional phenomena of experiencing.

A: It is akin to a poised posture, position, or prevailing attitude, like being at the prow of a ship that has only a solitary function despite the differing appearances of individual waves. Actually, the mind does it at a certain level all the time in that it notes multitudinous passing phenomena without pausing to react, memorize, or 'do' anything about them.

From the multitudinous input, the mind only pauses to select very few bits of information or data for attention and deliberate focus. The great majority of possible linear data is ignored even though it has registered and been observed. Attention is selective based on presumptive value, which is only transitory. By watching what the mind selects for attention, its proclivities become apparent and reveal the sources of attraction and aversion. By relinquishment of the propensity to project either desire or aversion, all becomes of equal value when devoid of projected specialness.

This style can be seen demonstrated in nature by a bird poised high over a shoreline where it positions itself to effortlessly take advantage of the ocean breezes. Its wings barely move and merely adjust to the wind with fine, subtle movements. Thus, it can tirelessly stay aloft for long periods of time.

Q: **But would not one be missing important observations or experiences?**

A: Again, 'important' and 'valuable' are indicative of editing. Without selection, all is of equal 'value' because the Source is from within as a consequence of innate existence itself. All is equally perfect, and the intrinsic beauty and perfection of all that exists radiate forth effortlessly.

With refusal to project values, all becomes of equal value by virtue of its existence and the emergence of Creation by which form is an expression of innate formlessness of Oneness. Perception focuses on linear uniqueness and differences and therefore on separation. The Self is all-inclusive.

The ego, by projection of presumptive value, sees beauty only selectively and bases it on the linearity subserved by expectations of aesthetics. Without editing, the intrinsic beauty of all that exists radiates forth as an innate quality of existence itself. In ordinary life, this observation tends to become obscured due to the sheer overwhelming quantity of stimuli. One purpose of art is to select almost any particular subject for focus and put it on 'stop' so its innate beauty and perfection as an expression of 'what it is' stand forth. This process reveals the presence of essence behind form.

Love has this characteristic as well, and the familiar becomes imbued with value because its inner worth has already been ascertained. By this process, familiar things become 'dear' and treasured, even if only a favorite pair of old slippers. To the Self, everything becomes endeared, not because it is 'mine', but because it 'is'.

Q: The method described is tantamount to eclipsing and precluding the 'experiencer' edge of the ego as the predominant focus of interest and psychic energy.

A: Its function can be bypassed, and therefore its editing

process is no longer valued. What is devalued tends to disappear. Awareness is a quality of consciousness itself that is not encumbered by having to 'do' anything. It just 'is' and by virtue of its innate capacity, apprehends essence *directly*. The Presence of Divinity as Self is effortless. It 'knows' as a quality of identity so there is no necessity to process a relationship between a 'this' and a 'that', or an 'I' and an 'it'. The Reality that is revealed by relinquishment of identification with the experiencer/processor edge of the ego cannot be easily described in words. The subjective awareness of existence is an unedited a priori primary knowingness beyond languaging. Its Source is the Self and not, as the ego believes it to be, the experiencer aspect of the self.

Q: Then there really is no 'razor' or 'edge'.

A: That analogy has pragmatic value until it is no longer serviceable or useful. It is like having a boat to cross a stream for a transition, but it serves no further function. That is common to all spiritual practices and techniques.

In the Presence of Divinity, there is no point to spiritual practices anymore than there would be to using the oars once the other shore has been reached. Like all denotative terms, the 'edge' disappears into the new linearity of the Oneness of the Self/Divinity. There is no personal self that witnesses the Ultimate Reality because the Knower and the Known dissolve into Identity. The term 'edge' denotes the interface of the processor/experiencer quality, which is an artificial separation. Another depiction, which again may seem ambiguous, is to say that everything is, by virtue of its own existent reality, already its own reflection.

Q: Contemplation then facilitates the break-through of discernment of essence from perception?

A: Contemplation allows the process to become the consequence of contextualization rather than focus. The process is more akin to the ephemeral. In practice, it is defocused as a consequence of intention. It is nonmanipulative. Spiritual techniques ripen and mature with reflection and then become effortlessly like 'second nature'—easy and natural. It is not something new to be gained or mastered but instead a natural propensity and capacity of consciousness as awareness and identity of the Knowingness of the Self. The Self is the inner Teacher whose qualities need only be noted and appreciated.

Q: Questions that stem from the ego arise as specific thoughts and inquiries. The Self expresses more as subtle inclinations that are not really verbal and explicit.

A: The ego would not know what questions to ask as its values and style of information gathering operate via other mechanisms. It can be seen that real questions arise spontaneously. It is as though the answers are already present but desire the finality of declaration to endorse clarification. It is a consequence of the unfolding process that encounters doubts. The process is also like the formal recognition of that which is already known but not enunciated. Everyone already at a certain level knows that they 'are'; the ego then quibbles about the details of definition, but the Self is not fooled by the ruse. All false identifications can be dropped in an instant with the willingness to surrender all mentalization to God.

Enlightenment is the consequence of a major shift of content and identification. The experiencer focus is like a screen that veils Reality and drops of its own accord when the props are removed. This is the consequence of surrendering the will to God. The sense of reality of the self was actually due solely to the underlying presence of the Self.

Q: **Languaging is for communication of information. When utilized in the spiritual realm, it eventually comes to an impasse that is frustrating. The mind wants to keep on mentalizing about it.**

A: Language is denotative by its specificity and linearity, but it also has nonverbal implication and reference that is its subjective quality as well. Thus, eventually a teaching becomes nonverbal and is conveyed via the nonlinear field of that level of consciousness whereby the knowingness is innate to the field itself. That is the value of the presence of a Teacher whose energy field is like a catalyst. The high energy field of the Self is already present in the student. It does not have to be acquired but only activated, which is a consequence of positive karmic potentiality.

CHAPTER 8

Allness Versus Nothingness

Introduction

The mind's content is expressed in linear form, such as concepts, ideas, images, and concordant emotionality. By spiritual endeavor, these are surrendered and thereby de-energized. At some point, an apprehension may arise that the 'self' is being obliterated and therefore, "I will no longer be me." Even further, the fear may be that one will cease to exist, which arises as the classic fear of nonexistence or nothingness. Understandably, the thought is that if the 'I' consists of just programs, and they are surrendered, will not the 'I' disappear also? Thus, it is important to understand the meaning of 'Void', especially so in view of the pervasiveness of the lack of full understanding of the term from various Buddhist texts and other writings, such as the pathway of negation described in the *Zen Teaching of Huang Po* (cal. 850). Subsequent to the quoted teachings, Huang Po continued to evolve to consciousness level 960, as was discussed in *Transcending the Levels of Consciousness*.

The Void

By the pathway of negation, a dedicated devotee may encounter the phenomenon of Voidness/Nothingness. This occurs at approximately consciousness level 850. The Void is seemingly complete and sufficient unto itself, as well as being impressive by virtue of its stillness and peace, along with the absence of ideation or any other form of linearity. "Surely," the devotee believes, "this is the state of Enlightenment," as the condition is still, peaceful, truly void, and not limited to time or space. The Void is also free of emotions or perceptions as it is nonlinear and thereby devoid of such options. This state is also eulogized by advanced students, i.e., "arhats" (cal. 800), who erroneously believe that the Void is the ultimate state of Enlightenment.

It is apparent that if Nothingness were the Ultimate Reality, there would be no one to report it for the observer would also be void. Thus, its being reported represents that consciousness itself is still present by awareness of the phenomenon.

The error arises twofold: (1) Misunderstanding the Buddha's teachings due to the lack of an explanation of terms and, (2) misidentification of Love as a bondage and a limitation. This latter arises from confusing personal, limited emotional love (between a 'me' and a 'you') with Divine Love, which is, in contrast, a nonlinear unconditional quality of Divinity, without subject or object.

Divine Love is an all-inclusive field, and its quality is unforgettable, as anyone who has ever had a near-death experience knows. It is intrinsically truly ineffable, and its presence is like a meltingness in its exquisite, experiential totality. There is nothing in worldly life that even comes close to it. It is profoundly gentle, yet infinitely powerful by virtue of its intrinsic infinite strength.

Innate to the Presence as Love is the quality of timelessness/foreverness. Even a brief moment of the Presence in earthly time is realized via the Self to be eternal. This is an unmistakable hallmark. Therefore, to have Known the Real for even a few brief moments of clock time is to know it forever.

The confusion about the Buddha's teachings is due to misinterpreting the concept of 'no thing' (void of linearity) to mean the voidness of Nothingness (nonexistence). Without Divine Love, it would indeed truly be Nothingness, and, paradoxically, nonexistence would then be a hypothetically possible 'reality'. 'Nothingness' is its own level, which is still incomplete as it lacks the Infinite Love that is the hallmark and major quality of Divinity. Its limitation is also indicated by its calibratable level of 850.

In this lifetime, the Void returned at age three when, out of the state of Nothingness, there was the sudden awareness of Existence that emerged spontaneously out of the voidness of Nothingness. Suddenly, there was the shocking presentation of the return of experiential existence and thus appeared the polarities of the duality of the Ultimate Truth as Nothingness versus Allness. Many years later, a rededication to the pathway of negation returned via the incessant desire to reach the core of Ultimate Truth, which again led to the Void. This time, however, there had already been the experience of the Presence, with its profound quality of timeless Love, and upon reentering the Void, the pathway of negation was refused. Consequently, the source of the prior error was discovered and thus was correctable by the recognition that Love is an innate quality of Divinity. It is, in fact, the primary quality of the Presence.

The basic error is due to confusing personal emotional love with Divine Love and negating love as an attachment, emotionality, specialness associated with dependence, and desire. Therefore, love is not really the problem, but its emotionalization as an interpersonal desire and attachment is the bondage to be surrendered.

While the above may seem premature or even irrelevant, at some time in the future, it may well arise. The pace of spiritual evolution is not controlled by convenience. The major barriers may suddenly disappear because their underpinnings have been eradicated and transcended.

Another reason to know about this now is to reduce the ubiquitous fear of the unknown that is either conscious or unconscious in spiritual seekers. Reassurance can be found by calibrating the levels of truth of the various teachers and teachings. The trap of the Void is an error that can be transcended by virtue of information. The Self knows the Ultimate Reality by virtue of identity; it is it. The Self thereby recognizes the Presence.

The Allness of Divinity

There is uncertainty about the alleged nature and reality of God, by whatever name Divinity is termed. Doubt frequently arises about the validity of personal spiritual experiences. It is therefore beneficial to review the innate qualities of Divinity that are irreducible and confirmable throughout time by determining consciousness calibration levels.

1. Divinity is nonlinear, impartial, nonjudgmental, and beyond partiality or selective favoritism.
2. Divinity is not capricious, judgmental, or subject to the limitations of presumptive human emotions. Divine Love, like the sun, is unconditional. Limitation is a consequence of the ego.
3. The justice of God is an automatic consequence of

the omnipotence and omniscience of Divinity. God does not 'do', 'act', or 'cause', but 'is'. The quality of Divinity radiates as an infinite field of power by which all that exists is automatically aligned by 'what' it is and has become. Each soul/spirit thus gravitates by virtue of its innate destiny to its own level, just as does a cork in the sea or an iron filing in an electromagnetic field.

4. Divinity is Absolute Dominion by virtue of its innate quality of infinite power, which is far beyond force. Force is a tool of positionality and control and is limited. Power is infinite strength. Because it is the very source of power as Divine Self, there is no need to seek it.

5. Within the All-Powerful, All-Presence of Divinity, all that exists aligns itself. This adjustment is the consequence of spiritual choice. Freedom is innate to Divine Justice.

6. The omniscience and omnipotence of Divinity, expressed as the infinite field of consciousness, is verifiable by consciousness research calibration techniques that confirm realities up and down the entire scale of possibility. All thoughts, actions, and decisions imprint upon the infinite field of consciousness, which is beyond time and location. By this imprint, justice is guaranteed.

Fear of God

This can be a block to spiritual progress as concepts and beliefs about Divinity arise, including gross misconceptions and false teachings. (The depictions of God by some religious groups amazingly calibrate as low as 20, and other presumable 'gods' abound that calibrate far below 200.) Each calibratable level of consciousness has concordant concepts and beliefs about Divinity. For people brought up in traditional Western or Near-Eastern religions, the fear of an anthropomorphic, angry, vengeful, punitive God recurs and thus emerges as a fear of God instead of reverence and respect for God. The truth of these numerous belief systems is easily obtained by consciousness calibration techniques, such as were reported in the latter chapters of *Truth vs. Falsehood*.

Fallacious teachings about God, especially those that calibrate very low, derive from primitive myths or from lower astral levels, many of which commonly have ostensible gods and prophets of limited regions that have many strange and bizarre characteristics. It is therefore wise to respect teachers and teachings of a high calibration and to avoid those below 200, about which scripture advises, "Do not go there."

Spiritual Evolution and the Problem with Specialness

Sometimes personal ego limitations are transcended, but the ego is clever and seeks to survive by incorporating spiritual concepts that thereby create what is known as the 'spiritual ego'. It may display itself by feeling superior to others, or more pure, or that it calibrates higher. Sometimes the ego's vanity is simply the wish to be considered 'spiritual'. Another trap of spiritual vanity is intellectual vanity, which is exhibited by the accumulation of a great deal of information and data about the details of religious and spiritual groups and their evolution over time. To know 'about' spiritual truth, however, is not the same thing as 'knowing' it, much less 'becoming' it.

Another variety of specialness is that with spiritual evolution, the capacity to love and radiate that field increases, which is attractive to others who misinterpret it as personal love. Thus, infatuation may be a temptation, and seduction has been the downfall of many unwary teachers who had a high calibration level early in their careers but then showed very severe decreases later on. It is necessary to recognize that each calibratable level of consciousness does not denote 'better than' those that precede it but is merely a stage of evolution. Each level is 'different from' the others, but at each level, excellence is its own hallmark.

The safeguards that protect one along the way from the temptations that arise consist of forewarning plus humility, gratitude, and, importantly, respect. One becomes grateful for the truth and its fruits and respectful of its origin. The integrous are also respectful of the possible pitfalls and temptations that may be encountered; therefore, this respect is reflected by alertness to such limitations. Humility is paradoxically a quality of respect. It is also wise to respect even the ego itself, for without its efforts over great eons of time, one would not have even survived long enough to seek to transcend it. It is a mistake to set up the ego as one's enemy to be conquered. It is more profitable to merely adopt it as a pet and melt it with compassion. Whatever the ego did in the past was because, like a puppy, it just did not know better. There is no profit in denouncing it as evil. To denounce it is to get stuck in the polarity/duality of good and evil rather than viewing it as a limitation. There is also no profit in personalizing it. Even the ego that 'should have known better' actually did not, or it would not have made an error.

Section Two

The Discussion

CHAPTER 9

Dialogues

Truth is sufficient unto itself, but its explanation and description are hampered by the fact that the appropriate languaging includes concepts and expressions that are unfamiliar in daily life. However, words also carry meaning and significance with associated effects (feelings) that bring up associated memories. The majority of literature about Self-Realization/Enlightenment arises from ancient teachings, with additions over the centuries by well-known sages.

The limitations that arise from traditional literature, especially from ancient times, is that the original truth conveyed was sometimes misunderstood and misinterpreted, especially when it was handed down verbally for centuries before being written. In addition, at the time the information was passed on orally, much of it was conveyed in a nonverbal and subtle manner, such as gestures, facial expressions, emphasis, volume, tone and cadence of voice, and body language. At times, all of these are more important than the actual verbalization. The style of teaching is also reflective of the teacher's intuitive estimate of the audience's capacity for comprehension.

A modern clarification and explanation are therefore of value, as well as consciousness calibration of the level of truth expressed. Lectures also tend to be didactic, and therefore, the question-and-answer periods at the end of the lectures are favored by many students. Some meanings and implications are best elucidated by the recontextualization of consequence, humor, paradox, and ambiguity. The questions and answers tend to be less detached, more informal, and less intellectually challenging.

Q: What is the purpose of spiritual writing?

A: To provide authenticated information that is not only verifiable but also experientially pragmatically useful. First, curiosity and the intellect have to be satisfied; there is a hunger for spiritual information. When it is not satisfied by the availability of valid information, the hunger creates a market for spurious spirituality that becomes popularized but is not serviceable to the student because it is based on imagination.

Much valid information is available but it retains the flavor and languaging of foreign cultures and obscure terminology, such as Sanskrit terms. When these are translated into English, they still seem archaic and reflective of ethnicity and foreign cultures and times. For example, the religious/cultural controversy that arose around the teachings of Meister Eckhart is not really comprehensible today because it has lost its historical context.

The primary purpose of a spiritual teaching is to provide reliable information in such a way as to be of practical service and inspiration and to affirm spiritual truth by subjective declaration. It is necessary that students be well informed in order to be able to proceed successfully and safely on their way. Guidelines are like principles of discovery, for that which is sought is already within.

Q: Notable in your writings and lectures is the absence of doctrine or citing of ecclesiastical authority.

A: Truth stands on its own. Scriptural references are

primarily for amplification or familiarity. The inner pathway is experiential and not intellectual. It does not require glamorization, amplification, resort to authoritarianism, or any other manipulation to try to impress the student.

Historically, no method was available to verify authenticity other than formal ecclesiastical approval. For example, in the Far East, authenticity was often inferred by reference to the material as a product of the authority of a lineage of sages. Due to the statistical rarity of the enlightened condition, any information about it was considered valuable as well as unique or special.

At the present time, an objective means of identification and validation of truth is now available through the method of consciousness calibration. Thus, it is no longer necessary to just depend on reputation, ecclesiastical authority, official 'imprimatur', hearsay, or public image. The chances for being misled are now far less. The mind, on its own, is an unreliable guide. It is easily misled by glamour, reputation, and popularity, with their associated enthusiasm and emotionality. The packaging or promotion of belief systems or teachers has no relationship to the value of the ingredients.

Q: **Who is the writer of your works or the speaker at lectures?**
A: The question itself is in error. It is better to ask 'what' rather than 'who'. In Reality, there is no 'who' but instead a suprapersonal quality or capacity that is autonomous and spontaneous. Intention catalyzes potentiality's becoming actuality. The

Reality/Source is the Teacher within, which is the Presence of the Self. Verbalization is the consequence of the utilization of the intellectual capacity of mind to subserve Mind. The dominion is that of Mind to which verbalized mind is merely a pragmatic tool. The Knowingness is nonlinear but its elucidation is linear for purposes of human communication. However, a simultaneous nonverbal level of communication occurs that facilitates comprehension by the listener. This is so via written works and even more so in the teacher's actual presence.

In the Teacher, the Knower is the Known. In ordinary mentation, the known and the knower are separate. In a Teacher, the duality of the Knower does not exist because they are the same by virtue of identity. The Self gives the answer to questions. It does not hear from an 'other'. The Knower/Self is the initiator/source of the speaker.

For example, by analogy, if we ask the cat, "What is it like to be a cat?" it would be puzzled. It just is what it is and has no need to objectify itself as a discernible object, so the cat replies saying, "What does 'cat' mean?"

We answer, "You."

The cat responds, "Oh, so that is what I am, or is that what I am called?"

We answer, "A cat is what you are called because that is what you are."

"Oh," says the cat, "but what does that mean?"

So we read to the cat what is written about cats in the encyclopedia.

The cat replies, "That is all very interesting, but it hasn't anything to do with who I am. I don't experience myself as a cat. I experience myself as 'me'." The cat continues, "Please explain what it is to be a 'me.' What is it like to be a human?"

We could only reply, "To be a 'me'."

"Thank you," says the cat, "now I understand what it is to be a cat. All I have to do is just be 'me'."

Thus we can see that the cat is both enlightened and of Divine origin, for 'to know that you *are*' is the crux of sentient life. That cat is happy and content just because it *is*. It has awareness/consciousness and is therefore perfect.

Q: Are 'experiencing' and 'awareness' different qualities?

A: The question leads to the interesting discovery that below consciousness level 200, there is the experiencing of life processes, but there is not yet the conscious awareness of existence. Thus, a frog experiences frog life but it is not aware yet that it is or has existence or beingness.

Both animal and human life change quality at consciousness level 200, where life becomes aware of its existence in the manner that it is. This is a remarkable difference that is demonstrated in the distribution of the levels of consciousness in the animal kingdom as well as in human life. It could be said that life is not valued for its own sake below consciousness level 200, and therefore, the worth of the lives of others is not valued for its own sake either. It is only beyond consciousness level 200 that concern for the well-being and value of the lives of 'others' really arises. Thus, below 200, the lifestyle is self-centered in both humans and animals.

Q: In the spiritual literature, 'one-pointedness of mind' is considered not only important but also a prerequisite for meditation or other spiritual practices.

A: That is simply the skill of concentration and unswerving volitional focus. It is like keeping one's eye of awareness focused on the road while driving. It means to refuse distractions. The unskilled, unsafe driver multifunctions by playing the radio, petting the dog, and eating a sandwich as he or she talks on the cell phone and reads billboards while driving. One-pointedness is like a skilled professional driver who knows he will get fired from the job for having even one accident, no matter how seemingly trivial. The willingness to establish the capacity for focused attention arises out of spiritual intention, which results in identification with the nonlinear field rather than linear content.

In much of spiritual work, the question is not whether one is able but whether one is willing. For example, one is faced with the temptation of desire.

Q: Could it be surrendered?

A: Yes, but will it be? Yes/no. The excuse given is, "I can't." Then we ask, "If a loaded gun were pointed at your head to comply or else die, could you?" The answer, of course, is "yes," because now one *will* do it. Thus, one really could have done it all along. Devotion means undistracted focus and alignment without equivocation. It represents determination and fixity of purpose and is merely inner discipline reinforced by decision and inspiration.

Q: The ego/mind and its emotions and feelings seem so strong and habitual.

A: True. Thus, it takes more than just a good idea to 'get spiritual' in order to transcend them. The force of instincts and negative emotions calibrates below 200. Above 200, one has the power of courage, the nonresistance of neutrality, and by the 300s, there are faith, enthusiasm, and willingness to which, in the 400s, are added intelligence, education, and the guidance of the intellect. At level 500, there is an important shift of paradigm, and values move from the tangible to the intangible, aided by the transformative quality of Love. Devotion is a commitment to Love as a guiding principle, reinforced by choice and the will. By surrender of the personal will and invocation, there is the intervention of Divine Will (the Self) invoked by alignment with spiritual purpose. With Divine assistance, the impossible becomes possible. Even that which is most prized by the ego/mind can actually be surrendered.

One-pointedness of mind means to focus on the crest of the wave of witnessing/experiencing plus being willing to surrender perceived loss or gain. That is the primary skill that is needed.

Q: How should one envision spiritual work?

A: The process is one of discovery and is thus directed within. It is by influence of the Self that spiritual endeavor becomes chosen as a life goal. It is primarily a decision.

Q: But cannot spiritual commitment and endeavor be disruptive to one's customary lifestyle?

A: Modification is ordinarily sufficient, at least in the beginning. Intensity of focus may bring about changes that are seen as disruptive; however, major life changes also occur as a result of lesser ambitions, such as changes in relationships, occupation, locality, illness, or other life circumstances.

Q: People often have a stereotyped image and expectation of what a spiritual teacher should look and sound like—usually with robes, a pious manner, and so forth.

A: The teaching style occurs spontaneously of its own. It is sometimes confrontive to the ego, which likes to go on and on circuitously. The information that has been provided beforehand is lengthy and detailed. To institute it, however, is a different matter. When resistance is confronted and made conscious by challenge, it frequently loses its attraction. A shift in the balance of energy is sometimes all that is required. Occasionally, without prodding, the ego tends to drag its feet or waste time chasing its tail by asking rhetorical questions. To hear 'enough is enough' can assist the letting go of such programs.

Humor results from shifting context by which absurdity reveals itself. Humor is also confrontive to positionality—to laugh at oneself or help others to do so relieves conflict and stress. Humor is therapeutic and cathartic. It also minimalizes fear, anger, or resentment. Mistakes keep us humble and therefore teachable. Abruptness is sometimes necessary to spiritual economy to save time and energy.

Q: **Spiritual economy?**

A: Yes. It is necessary to develop respect for spiritual endeavor. "Straight and narrow is the path, waste no time or effort." Precision is discipline that is innate to serious commitment. Some students may yet be in a period of exploration, but once one gets the 'fire in the belly,' the urge to reach God becomes like a drivenness or relentless drive, or even, in the eyes of the world, a 'madness.' From that point on, there is no patience for amusement or diversion. It depends on decision, will, the level of consciousness, and karmic propensities. As it gets more intense, the love for God and of God allows no delay.

CHAPTER 10

Spirituality and the World

Serious inner spiritual work may sound tedious and demanding (to the ego), but is exciting to the spirit, which is eager to return home. Consciousness innately seeks its source. In so doing, it encounters obstacles from which it may periodically retreat, and this may result in periods of reflection and reorientation. Periods of resistance or even dismay are normal and to be expected. Their resolution is often the consequence of recontextualization.

Although the personal will and motivation, plus the mind and intellect, are strong tools, in and of themselves they do not have the strength to disassemble the ego because they are part and parcel of it. However, once a seeker becomes devoted, the strength of the spiritual Will via the Presence of the Self supplies the necessary power.

The inner work that arises as a consequence of commitment to Enlightenment is at times admittedly experientially difficult or even arduous. Although this is due to resistance, the sheer seeming difficulty may provoke discouragement or a temptation to abandon the goal. This, however, is also to be expected and therefore merely included in the material to be processed.

Contemplation results in insights consequent to redefinition and recontextualization. In the meantime, other spiritual practices continue, such as meditation, prayer, service, and spiritual group activities. The letting-go process encounters inner fixations and addictions to various ego pay-offs and lures. Sometimes periods of retreat are helpful, and at other times, active involvement in spiritual activities is beneficial. Frequently, the seemingly impossible obstacle mysteriously and spontaneously disappears and resolves itself.

Aside from ordinary resistances that are innate to the ego itself and therefore not really 'personal', there are inherited propensities as a consequence of karmic factors. These can sometimes be intuited either by prayer or even by specific investigation, such as with past-life recall techniques. Persistent patterns indicate that the source of the problem is still unconscious. A useful uncovering technique is to presume that there is a repressed aspect in the unconscious, and that the unconscious is not only personal but also collective, described by Carl Jung as the "collective unconscious." Thus, certain problems are merely the karmic inheritance of being human.

In practice, for example, if other people persistently seem cruel or rude, it may be beneficial to forgive and pray for help for that hidden aspect in oneself that is cruel, rude, and unforgiving. These aspects can be accepted in that they are impersonal to some extent, yet one is responsible for them as a participant human being. For example, if others seem selfish or stingy, pray for that aspect in oneself that is that way. It is often surprising to discover that there is such a deeply repressed hidden trend that may well be just a consequence of human inheritance and experience.

Asceticism

This is a useful practice at various periods by which one accomplishes detachment from the senses and their endless search for pleasure and sensation. Success brings a sense of accomplishment. The senses search for pleasure via amusement, excitement, and the lure of enticements that increase appetite and desire. Their origination was in the animal phase of evolution and instinctual in origin. A useful technique to overcome them is to delay gratification of sensory desires, and before seeking to satisfy them, surrender either resisting or desiring the sensations themselves, for example, the craving feeling, and not label them. Actually, one does not experience 'hunger', which is actually a nominalization, a label, and a diagnosis. The actual physical sensations are merely that and not a 'need'. When ignored and surrendered, they recede and fade away. Therefore, if there is a desire, ignore the desire and focus on the actual sensations themselves. In a surprisingly few minutes, the craving recedes. Another trick is to only eat when not hungry and to eat prophylactically in anticipation so as to avoid the resurgence of hunger later. This process is akin to deprogramming Pavlovian conditioning.

Asceticism can be a discipline that is introduced into routine daily life on a modified basis and maintained as a lifestyle. It leads to economy of time, energy, money, and other resources. It is freeing to discover how little one actually requires in order to subsist, function, and enjoy life.

Renunciation

This is a traditional type of spiritual retreat from the world and sometimes done for variable periods, such as even just a weekend. True renunciation, however, in its full understanding, is the application of renunciation to the payoffs of the ego itself and the identification of self with body, emotions, or mind. By renunciation and dissociation through surrender and relinquishment, it is discovered that none of them are 'me' or even 'mine'. In actuality, they are autonomous functionalities. One can renounce the seeking of gain or worldliness as well as the seeking of pleasure, excitement, or titillation. One can renounce the assumption that perceptions are reality or essence. By renunciation, one can withdraw invested emotional energy and interest in the world without physically having to depart from it.

Formal renunciation as a lifestyle has been and still is an option for devotees for whom such a major decision is appropriate. Such communities have prevailing requirements, and monastic orders are well known (Trappists, Dominicans, Benedictines, Buddhists, the Ramakrishna Order, etc.). Most require vows of allegiance and serious commitment.

The World

The planet is part of the physical universe and thereby subject to its transitions and evolutionary phenomena. Volcanic eruptions, earthquakes, tsunamis, forest fires, and floods have been recurring over the eons of time, including the impact of giant meteors that filled the sky with dust and smothered all of life. It is therefore naïve to assume that phenomena are consequent to mankind's follies, frailties, failures, or religious belief systems. So-called 'end times' phenomena are redundant, both before and subsequent to the emergence of Homo sapiens. Numerous are the prophets and prophesies that have come and gone. When the great meteors hit and blanked out the sky, mankind was not yet even born. Contextualizing earthly phenomena as evidence of the 'wrath of God' is primi-

tive, naïve, and an anthropomorphic distortion of the
Reality of Divinity. God is not emotionally imbalanced
or needful of psychological help, spiritual counseling,
or anger-management classes

Even if all these mystifications were true, of what
interest is it, anyway, to the individual seeker? If life on
earth is to end in either a few years, or in the year 6017
or 8095, so what? What does it really have to do with
one's own level of spiritual evolution? The wise
renounce public hysteria or mass suicides because a
comet is sighted somewhere in space. Even if an 'end
times' catastrophe were to happen, it would seem to be
a better decision to pray rather than kill oneself inasmuch as one's death would be a certainty, and suicide
carries karmic consequences.

The evolution of human consciousness expresses
its cultural and social changes that, in turn, reflect
karmic propensities and inheritances of whole
groups of people over great periods of time. In the
East, karma is a matter of ordinary acceptance, but
that is not so in the Western world, which even lauds
unaccountability and irresponsibility as promoted by
moralistic relativism.

By consciousness calibration research, it is demon-
strable that every thought, action, word, or deed is
recorded forever, beyond time, in an infinite field of
consciousness for eternity. It is affirmed by consciousness research that everyone is accountable to the universe (Divinity) by virtue of Divine Justice. Thus, everyone already has a calibratable level of consciousness from
the very moment of birth. Life is neither accidental nor
arbitrary, nor is it based on anarchy. The stratification of
levels of consciousness are influential by virtue of their

prevailing, powerful 'attractor fields' (see *Power vs. Force*) whereby like goes to like by attraction and alignment.

Q: As a spiritual person, what is our responsibility in relation to world events?

A: This depends on one's current prevailing level of consciousness. Confusion arises from mixing the levels. To act according to the spiritual principles of mercy, forgiveness, love, and compassion applies at all levels, of course, but how these are interpreted and what they are understood to signify regarding action depends on perception and degree of spiritual maturity.

Earthly life affords maximum karmic opportunity to not only acquire 'good' karma but also to undo negative karma. For example, whole populations and groups have accumulated both positive and negative spiritual consequences as the result of barbaric savagery, just as they do in today's headlines. Thus, there are spiritual 'debts' as well as benefits.

While it is commonly believed that Christianity does not teach karma, that is not true. It does indeed, but it merely does not use the specific term. Christianity teaches that sin and virtue have very different consequences for the soul after death. These include the karmic alternatives of not only heaven or hell, but also purgatory. In addition, a traditional teaching is that man was 'born in sin' due to the fall of Adam and Eve and is thus karmically affected by succumbing to temptation and refusing obedience to God. Subsequently, God's mercy is represented by the presentation of a savior born for the sake of man's redemption.

As Jesus said, "None get to heaven but by Me."

In Buddhism, there is the Lotus Land (Heaven) where an aspect of the Buddha speaks as an advocate. From another culture in a different time, Krishna also taught that those who worship and love God by whatever name are "Mine and dear to Me." This is the same teaching presented in the Ninety-first Psalm.

The primary spiritual gift of human existence is the opportunity that by the option of one's own free will, Divinity may be chosen or rejected by whatever name God is known. Thus, human life and the permission to incarnate as a human are great gifts in themselves, as was pointed out by the Buddha.

Affairs of the world are perceived and interpreted in accordance with one's level of consciousness. Therefore, the world may appear to be tragic, sad, miserable, or fearful, or it may, on the contrary, seem tempting, exciting, and challenging. In the high 500s, it is viewed with compassion and seen as beauty. In the 600s, it is seen as peaceful, and then, in the 700s, as Ramana Maharshi said, "The world you 'see' (i.e., perception) does not even exist; therefore, surrender it to God."

Human life is a major spiritual opportunity for consciousness to evolve and even reach Enlightenment. It is an expression of the gift of life, through which one can eventually realize the Self. Worldly temporal life is transitory and brief, but its consequences are very long term. It is therefore best to treasure the opportunity with gratitude. Spiritual endeavor is, in and of itself, an expression of appreciation for that gift of life.

Q: But what about the vicissitudes of life?

A: Each has a hidden gift. Sometimes it is an opportunity to undo past suffering brought to others. Sometimes the suffering is due to resistance and is a consequence of the ego's personal will and therefore needful of surrender. An overall attitude of humility is very helpful, and by surrender, the hidden gift is revealed. How a specific situation is handled depends on how it is conceptualized and contextualized, and therefore, what it seems to 'mean'.

Q: Is a given event an opportunity, or is it a temptation?

A: From the view of consciousness itself, one might say that the world is really amorphous, and that all meaning is a derivation of projected value, perceptual interpretation, and mentation. If the predominant lesson that is arising at a certain level of consciousness is nonattachment to success, desire, or pleasure, the temptations of the world could be refused. Also, a surrender of positionalities might result in deciding to actually surrender the world to God. A person in a similar situation might see a worldly event as a call for selfless service. Another might view it as a call for taking an integrous stand or, on the contrary, refusing to take any position and may be seeing it as a reflection of perception and any decision as a vanity of egoism.

There is no point to jumping in to 'save the world' when the perceived world is merely an illusion of projected values, presumptions, and interpretations. The integrous student chooses what appears to be the highest, and to evolve spiritually is actually the greatest gift one can give the world. This is done by virtue of what one is and not just by what one does. The truly great have come and gone, and what they left behind was the consequence of what they were and had become.

Q: Thus, renunciation is an internal, not an external, event.

A: Noninvolvement means to act without volitional gain. Actions are spontaneous and represent potentiality's expressing as actuality. The spiritual devotee has dedicated personal life to spiritual evolution and has aligned with Truth as a map for guidance. A common question to ask is, "Which option or direction would serve the highest good?" Those serve who also stand and wait. Sometimes the mind cannot tell the forest from the trees.

In decision-making, it is best to be aligned with context and the field instead of content. It is difficult at times to differentiate sacrifice from service. Consciousness at the level of awareness/witness/observer is free of involvement. If perfected, however, at a later time it may allow reparticipation because of noninvolvement consequent to surrender of attachments, attractions, or aversions. Actions may also represent karmic propensities, and the same course of action may actually have very different meanings and consequences in different individuals at different times and circumstances. Therefore, there is no supposed 'spiritual' way to be or attitudes to have about worldly events, as there are actually multiple options. It takes inner discipline and surrender of attitudes to not fall into the temptation of identifying with a position about world events.

The events of the world trigger responses based on perceptions. It is a great theater that invites expressions of perceptions, illusions, and projections of positionalities. One can either turn off the television and avoid it or see it as a major teaching tool. The panoramic events of the entire world unfold, representing the multitudinous expressions of the human ego; thus, the television is its ultimate game board. Perception may see this reflection of human-ego life as absurd, tragic, or comic. It can be seen as sad, pathetic, exiting, heartwarming, challenging, or alternately, as ridiculous. As the television news program says, "You decide."

The real question is, Who is the real 'you' that decides? That is the question to be answered by the spiritual student. The 'you' has multiple options and can choose any of them. Therefore, the world is kaleidoscopic-tragic-comic-nurturing-absurd-cruel-lovable-ugly-despicable-deplorable, none of the above, or just a transitory illusion. It is allegorical.

The spiritual advantage of modern life is that life experiences are speeded up via the media. In a very short time, one can witness what would have taken multiple lifetimes in previous eras where, for example, a whole lifetime could be limited to just the experience of a small space and limited role, such as that of a sheepherder or a village blacksmith. Now multiple lives, perspectives, circumstances, and conditions are presented

in succession, from grotesque crimes to corona-
tions, domestic family situations, major wars, and
world catastrophes.

Whether to take advantage of the television
display of the human ego or to ignore it and go
within are equally serviceable for it is one's intention that decides the outcome. Either way requires
compassion for self and others. A certain quantity
of suffering is impersonal and consequent to the
physicality of being born a human. Thus, the
Buddha exhorted followers to transcend the ego to
avoid rebirth, sickness, poverty, old age, and death.
The world and everything in it is transitory; therefore, to cling to it brings suffering. As a result, he
stressed detachment.

**Q: What about the popular exhortations to 'get
involved' and 'make a difference'?**

A: Compassionate attention, in and of itself, has an
unseen influence. The results of volitional action
are consequent to intention and the level of consciousness. Sometimes the world would benefit
more from benign noninvolvement. Great wars and
massive human disasters that go on for centuries
are the result of the ego's grandiose plans to be
involved and make a difference, from Genghis Khan
to Karl Marx, from Adolf Hitler to current terrorists.

Q: How to best serve the world?

A: Each individual's evolution of spiritual consciousness contributes to the progress of the consciousness level of all mankind. By uplifting the sea, all
ships afloat are lifted. The effect of actions that

emerge from compassion are the result of intention.

Human consciousness evolves through learning, which is often primarily experiential. It is usually presumptuous to assume the 'purpose' of witnessed human events. What is deemed appropriate is a consequence of perception and contextualization. Thus, whether action is appropriate or not is an option that reflects a prevailing level of consciousness rather than discernment of the Reality of essence.

Everyone is accountable and culpable in accordance with their own level of consciousness. Whether to 'get involved' or not reflects vanity or compassion is consequent to the overall field of both content and context. Action or nonaction is the spontaneous response of what has 'become' or 'is'. There is no prevailing rule of appropriate behavior because effects are consequent to intention.

Q: Choices are therefore based on presumption and appearance?

A: These are also aligned with stages of spiritual development and their overall intention. There are periods devoted to learning detachment and then periods devoted to transcending avoidance. Each has its temptations and attractions. The specifics of the dualities of each level of consciousness were discussed in *Transcending the Levels of Consciousness*.

Q: In addition to what appear to be worldly choices, are there also karmic influences and propensities?

A: Those factors contribute to the problems of choice for they influence understandings of meaning, significance, and implications of importance. Evolution leads to discovery that, in turn, reveals nuances, significances, and inferences for further exploration. That is the nature of transcendence by which many seeming paradoxes or conflicts spontaneously resolve due to overall alignment consequent to intention. The overall spiritual process is therefore concordant with a contemplative lifestyle that incorporates reflection and the development of discernment.

Q: **Would the overall consequences of intense inner spiritual focus tend to result in detachment and noninvolvement in the world?**

A: As a general trend, that is characteristic. As the ego's dominance of perception recedes, so does the appearance of the world and the mind's interpretations. Decisions are based on projected perceptions. Thus, the mind perceives endless illusions, including classifications based on judgments. Those that are interpreted as 'good' options are attractive to choice and agreement. Thus, all perceptions reflect content.

Patterns of conduct result from belief systems consequent to prevailing social/educational systems that are both explicit and implicit. Thus, 'duty calls' in both overt and subtle expressions. To adopt the pathway of devotional nonduality recontextualizes the obligation to the pursuit of Truth rather than worldly involvement and action. How best to serve the world is concordant with comprehension.

Q: **What is the most serviceable presumptive view of the world for a spiritual student/devotee/seeker?**

A: Presume that the world's actual 'purpose' is perfect and fully known only by God. See it as neutral overall but with the benefit that it provides optimal opportunity for spiritual growth and the evolution of consciousness. It is a school for enlightenment and the revelation of Divinity whereby consciousness/awareness reawakens to its Source. Thus, to pursue enlightenment in and of itself serves the world and God.

Q: **But what about war?**

A: This is a favorite question of spiritual students. War is the consequence of falsity, just as peace is the consequence of Truth. War has prevailed during ninety-three percent of human history. It is endemic to the ego. To be 'anti-war' is also an ego position that presumes omniscience. Therefore, it is more advanced to surrender the world and its wars to God.

To 'hate war' is merely another expression of hate, is it not? Better to love peace and come to nonjudgmental compassion for the world's wars and its karmically influenced participants. Would the protester rob fellow-suffering humans of the opportunity to undo negative karma and reach salvation?

Suffering and death are the consequences of the ego and its positionalities and perceptions. To best serve the world, seek Enlightenment and transcend illusions rather than contribute to them. Omniscience is a quality of Divinity, not of human perception. Watch that the spiritual ego does not become politicized. 'Do-gooderism' is a trap for the naïve and unwary. Be 'pro' God's will and Divine providence for the world and humanity. How best to 'serve the highest good' is concordant with the prevailing level of consciousness of the observer. There is no single answer for everyone.

CHAPTER 11

Teachers and Teaching

Introduction

The evolved Teacher historically has been the primary source of Truth and spiritual information. The function has been to inspire, inform, and convey information that is not obtainable via ordinary mind. The Teacher has been unique in that the Source of the Knowledge has been intrinsic rather than external. That the Source of the Knowingness is Self-effulgent and not the result of linear processing resulted in the use of the descriptive term 'mystic' to denote that the Source of the information is the Self, not the self or ordinary mind, education, or intelligence.

The Illumined State is also accompanied and distinguished by a concomitant radiance of a specific spiritual energy via the aura, which is often pictorially represented by the symbol of the halo to denote that the energy field is innately radiant. That energy field is a permanent marker which persists beyond time or location. It has become possible within the last decade to accurately calibrate the specific level of consciousness that is being displayed as a result of the emergence of a greater understanding of consciousness. Therefore, the calibratable level is the research confirmation of concordance with the degree and level of truth expressed. Currently, credibility is bulwarked by confirmable data that preclude reliance on just faith or reputation alone.

Enlightenment is a very definite state or condition that is self-revealing when the obstructions to its realization have been removed, just like the sun shines forth with the evaporation or disappearance of clouds.

The sun is likened to the Self in that it is self-effulgent and radiates the energy that is termed 'Illumination'.

The statistical infrequency of such a phenomenon in the human population tends to attract attention to the condition by virtue of not only its rarity but also its intrinsic value of uniqueness. The Teachings that ensue are a consequence of the condition itself and not of any personality. Because the process is not mental, emotional, or physical, it has been perceived as 'mystical', meaning mysterious or not within the province of the mind or intellect to comprehend via ordinary perception or conceptualization (i.e., nonlinear).

Subsequent to its original legitimate meaning, the term 'mystical' was inadvertently applied to other conditions that also were not comprehensible to reason in derivation, such as having visions, hearing voices, or other paranormal phenomena that were not familiar to ordinary mind. In contrast, there is a long-established tradition of mystical states often associated with the presumption of sainthood or highly aware states of consciousness. To make the differentiation between the truly mystical and the merely mysterious, it is well to be aware that the condition of Enlightenment or Self-realization is devoid of 'others', such as mysterious visitors, guides, messengers, visions, or voices, all of which one can quickly see are characteristic of linearity and therefore limitations.

The differentiation between a Divine messenger and a religious-content hallucination can be made by the technique of consciousness calibration. In Christianity, there is also the teaching of the 'challenging of spirits' to declare their allegiance to Jesus Christ as Savior. A demon or astral entity cannot do so.

The Functions of the Teacher

The primary function is that of declaration of the condition or state and thus affirmation of the Reality of its Source, traditionally called Divinity. The Presence is of a dimension different from that of ordinary experiencing and therefore requires a rather specific and unique type of languaging. It is of a Source beyond that of ordinary experiencing and is instead a quality of Reality devoid of linearity. That the Source of consciousness/awareness is simultaneously beyond even existence or nonexistence is impossible to language except by intuitive implication, for even the sun is a consequence of realities that are beyond and greater than the sun itself.

The linear manifest world (Creation) is itself an emergence from the nonlinear, which is depicted as the Unmanifest (the Godhead). The enlightened Teacher is therefore the example or confirmation within the visible, linear human domain of the Source, out of which Enlightenment and life itself manifest. An Enlightened Teacher is therefore the exemplification of the human potential as a demonstration within the visible world. The condition or state of the Enlightened Teacher represents the threshold at which the nonlinear Source might well be said to emerge from potentiality to actuality, much as a light bulb is a transformer of electrical energy into light. Although both light and electricity emanate from the same source, which is invisible, it is only the light that is visible. Thus, the enlightened sage is akin to a transformative agency by which the agent becomes visible and confirmable. This is then expressed as a function of the

Sage/Mystic as the witness who gives testimony to other dimensions of Reality that transcend the ordinary. The uniqueness is represented by the descriptive term 'ineffable'. The mystical state itself is an a priori development of a religion that then takes on the forms of description and explanation as perceived and contextualized by linear mentation. However, the condition or state of Enlightenment is one of 'no-mind'; thus, interpretation by mentation subtly eludes the Essence of the Reality itself.

As described, a primary function of the Teacher is to declare and describe the Truth and thus represent the Truth out of which the state of Enlightenment emerged. By declaration and description, the Teacher then radiates forth the accompanying spiritual energy of its origination, facilitating the transcendence of others to the enlightened state.

Confirmation and Concordance

The reemergence of the primordial potential state, in whatever time or culture, is always essentially the same, albeit with seeming differences in description that reflect the prevailing culture and its style of languaging at the time. Subsequent descriptions often include irrelevancies and extraneous aspects of the prevailing culture and times and contaminate the original teachings that, in and of themselves, are pristine and independent of people, places, or culture.

The Service of Enlightenment

The Teacher serves to communicate information that is of self-evident, intrinsic value to humankind. It is therefore stated openly and freely to all that its origination is by virtue of a Divine gift and is not personal. Because of the transcendent quality of the inner Reality, the sharing of the condition for its innate value is implicit to the nature of the gift itself. At times, various teachers, in order to emphasize the intrinsic value, may declare the value of the state or the condition to facilitate its recognition by means of education. This would be comparable to the effort of Sir Alexander Fleming subsequent to his discovery of penicillin, in that without explanation, the value of the discovery may have been overlooked, as would have its value as the springboard for the emergence of the pharmacology of antibiotics that subsequently saved the lives of millions of people.

Paradoxically, from the condition of 'no-mind' (Mind, or Consciousness itself), the limitations of ordinary mind, including intellect and reason, become apparent. Ordinary mind, with its linear, dualistic, emotionalized perceptions and limitations, is like the clouds in the sky that occlude the radiance of the sun. Thus, the way to clear the clouds can be clarified by a teacher who has successfully transcended the apparent obstacle course.

Potentiality manifests as actuality when conditions are favorable and includes being energized by intention. The Teacher thus serves not only as an instructor but also, by radiating the energy of the witness, facilitates the journey from the linear dimension to the unlimited nonlinear Reality hidden by illusion. The Ultimate Reality is of a different dimension, quality, and paradigm from that of 'experiencing'. Consequently, it is 'realized' rather than perceived, conceptualized, or experienced by virtue of the

Identity of the Knower and the Known.

Languaging and Teaching Style

The state of Enlightenment is expressed in a style that is concordant with the condition itself. Thus, statements are often declarative in form rather than semiconditional or prepositional, as it is in ordinary languaging. This is because the state itself is a primary condition that is not dependent on context and has no external qualifications or dependencies. The language therefore reflects what 'is' rather than what 'appears to be', which is operationally always semiconditional, dependent on both content and the proximate field. The state is unconditional and therefore so is its languaging, which is free of doubt or external dependencies. The reason for the above is that the Knowingness originates from the realm of Essence rather than from appearance and is therefore free of conditionalities, such as 'seems to be', 'appears to be', 'is described as', or 'is believed to be'. The nonlinear is confirmable but not 'provable', which is a linear process limited to the consciousness level of the 400s.

Without understanding this state, some statements made by a sage could be misidentified as being dogmatic or authoritarian, which they are not. The statements merely reflect certainty and authority by virtue of identity. By analogy, the only true authority about being a cat is that of the cat itself, by virtue of its being a cat. Thus, identity is authority by virtue of nondualistic Reality. The Teacher thus bypasses duality by virtue of identity with the Oneness of the Self, which is the true Teacher within the Teacher.

The 'Personage' or Persona of the Teacher

The inner Silence is mute, unmoving, silent, still, and all pervasive. It is all-inclusive and complete. If so destined, the Enlightened Teacher may continue to function on Earth, but that propensity is solely up to Divine Destiny. One reason there are so few enlightened teachers on the planet at any one time is that upon reaching Divine states, the majority merely transcend the body. That becomes an open, continuous option beyond consciousness level 600, again subject to influential factors that are unknown or indescribable.

To be of service, information has to be made available, and thus the Self activates the capacity of the Teacher to communicate by virtue of the reemergence of the persona/personage functionality that thereby interfaces with the world via mind/languaging faculties. Even though the mind is silent, speaking occurs spontaneously as a consequence of the proximate invitational field. The same spontaneity occurs via writing, which supports availability and access to information. As a result, information becomes accessible worldwide and transgenerational.

To a live audience, the persona becomes interactive as an autonomous agency that is simultaneously devoid of individuality or personhood. Thus, the speaker is a functionality and not a personality. The persona rapidly and autonomously adjusts to changes in a situation, but when inactivated, it is silent and nonexistent, just as silence prevails in the absence of sound. Communication therefore represents the activation of a potentiality. Similarly, activation of the body occurs autonomously and spontaneously in coordination with environmental situations.

Paradoxically, the option to depart from physicality remains an open potentiality.

The Nature of Communication

Spiritual truth represents nonlinear power and strength. Thereby, its expression may likewise be unadorned. The style of communication automatically tends to align with the goal of serviceability to the listeners and the capacity to comprehend and intuit the recognition of the innate reality of Truth. Sometimes there is elaboration of explanation, and at other times brevity, which serves economy of time and energy. Thus, the style of communication is an expression of the stewardship of that which is of value. Actually, it takes only 1/10,000th of a second to 'get' something for which one is ready by virtue of surrendering the gratification of personal intentions.

The Teacher is not motivated to convince anyone because acceptance is a privilege of freedom, nor is the Teacher interested in 'proving', persuading, proselytizing, or promoting. When the time is right, the apple falls from the tree. There is no need to shake it, intimidate it, or resort to cajolery. All occurs when it is propitious by virtue of intention, karmic propensities, and favorable conditions. All that evolves does so by the agency of the evolution of consciousness itself; thus, the Teacher represents fulfillment of potential.

Spiritual statements are valid at their calibrated level of Truth. The truths of formal religion can also be verified at the respective calibration levels. Religious truths are reinforced by ecclesiastical authority and formal acceptance as doctrine. Spiritual truth, on the other hand, relies on no external authority but stands on its own by virtue of its pristine origin. The invitation of spiritual pathways is to subjectively reaffirm those spiritual realities upon which the survival of humankind actually relies, knowingly or not.

Characteristics of Integrous Teachers and Teachings

That to which devotees trust their very souls should be verifiably trustworthy and integrous. Therefore, the basic essentials of researched and documented spiritual integrity, teachers, teachings, and organizations are reprinted here from *Truth vs. Falsehood* for convenience.

Identification and Characteristics of Spiritual Truth, Integrous Teachers, and Teachings

1. **Universality**: Truth is true at all times and places, independent of culture, personalities, or circumstances.
2. **Nonexclusionary**: Truth is all-inclusive, nonsecretive, and nonsectarian.
3. **Availability**: It is open to all; nonexclusive. There are no secrets to be revealed, hidden, or sold, and no magical formulas or 'mysteries'.
4. **Integrity of purpose**: There is nothing to gain or lose.
5. **Nonsectarian**: Truth is not the exposition of limitation.
6. **Independent of opinion**: Truth is nonlinear and not subject to the limitations of intellect or form.
7. **Devoid of Positionality**: Truth is not 'anti' anything. Falsehood and ignorance are not its enemies but merely represent its absence.

8. **No requirements or demands**: There are no required memberships, dues, regulations, oaths, rules, or conditions.

9. **Noncontrolling**: Spiritual purity has no interest in the personal lives of aspirants, or in clothing, dress, style, sex lives, economics, family patterns, lifestyles, or dietary habits.

10. **Free of force or intimidation**: There is no brainwashing, adulation of leaders, training rituals, indoctrinations, or intrusions into private life.

11. **Nonbinding**: There are no regulations, laws, edicts, contracts, or pledges.

12. **Freedom**: Participants are free to come and go without persuasion, coercion, intimidation, or consequences. There is no hierarchy; instead, there is voluntary fulfillment of practical necessities and duties.

13. **Commonality**: Recognition is a consequence of what one has become rather than a result of ascribed titles, adjectives, or trappings.

14. **Inspirational**: Truth eschews and avoids glamorization, seduction, and theatrics.

15. **Nonmaterialistic**: Truth is devoid of neediness of worldly wealth, prestige, pomp, or edifices.

16. **Self-fulfilling**: Truth is already total and complete and has no need to proselytize or gain adherents, followers, or 'sign up members'.

17. **Detached**: There is noninvolvement in world affairs.

18. **Benign**: Truth is identifiable along a progressive gradient. It has no 'opposite' and therefore no 'enemies' to castigate or oppose.

19. **Nonintentional**: Truth does not intervene or have

an agenda to propose, inflict, or promulgate.

20. **Nondualistic**: All transpires by virtue of intrinsic (karmic) propensity within the field by which potentiality manifests as actuality rather than by 'cause' and effect.

21. **Tranquility and Peace**: There are no 'issues' or partialities. There is no desire to change others or impose on society. The effect of higher energies is innate and not dependent on propagation or effort. God does not need help anymore than gravity needs the 'help' of an apple's falling off the tree.

22. **Equality**: This is expressed in reverence for all of life in all its expressions and merely avoids that which is deleterious rather than opposing it.

23. **Nontemporality**: Life is realized to be eternal and physicality to be a temporality. Life is not subject to death.

24. **Beyond proof**: That which is 'provable' is linear, limited, and a product of intellectualization and mentation. Reality needs no agreement. Reality is not an acquisition but instead is a purely spontaneous, subjective realization when the positionalities of the dualistic ego are surrendered.

25. **Mystical**: The origination of truth is a spontaneous effulgence, radiance, and illumination, which is the Revelation that replaces the illusion of a separate individual self, the ego, and its mentation.

26. **Ineffable**: Not capable of definition. Radical subjectivity is experiential. It is a condition that replaces the former. With this event, context replaces content, devoid of temporality and beyond time. Reality does not exist in time, nor of it, beyond it, nor outside of it, and it has no relationship to that

which is an artifice of mentation. It is therefore beyond all nouns, adjectives, or verbs, transitive or intransitive.

27. **Simplistic**: One sees the intrinsic beauty and perfection of all that exists beyond appearance and form.

28. **Affirmative**: Truth is beyond opinion or provability. Confirmation is purely by its subjective awareness; however, it is identifiable by consciousness calibration techniques.

29. **Nonoperative**: Truth does not 'do' anything or 'cause' anything; it is everything.

30. **Invitational**: As contrasted with promotional or persuasive.

31. **Nonpredictive**: Because Reality is nonlinear, it cannot be localized or encoded in restriction of form, such as secret messages, codes, numbers, and inscriptions, or hidden in runes, stones, the dimensions of the pyramid, the DNA, or the nostril hairs of the camel. Truth has no secrets. The Reality of God is omnipresent and beyond codification or exclusivity. Codes are indicative of man's imagination and not the capriciousness of Divinity.

32. **Nonsentimental**: Emotionality is based on perception. Compassion results from the discernment of truth.

33. **Nonauthoritarian**: There are no rules or dictates to be followed.

34. **Non-egoistic**: Teachers are respected but reject personal adulation or specialness.

35. **Educational**: Provides information in a variety of formats and ensures availability.

36. **Self-supporting**: Neither mercenary nor materialistic.

37. **Freestanding**: Complete without dependence on external or historical authorities.
38. **Natural**: Devoid of induced, altered status of consciousness or manipulations of energies by artificial exercises, postures, breathing, or dietary rituals, (i.e., nonreliance on form or physicality; no invoking of entities or 'others').
39. **Complete**: Devoid of exploitation or gain.

Spiritual Teachers

It is useful to calibrate the levels of consciousness of the teachers and associated literature. For practical convenience, many of the well-known are inserted here from *Truth vs. Falsehood*.

Following is a list of over one hundred well-known, respected teachers from various schools. They all calibrate over 460 (Excellence), and their works have withstood the test of time. The list, of course, is not complete and would include many others if space permitted.

Abhinavagupta	655	Dalai Lama (Tenzin Gyatso)	570
Acharya	480	de Chardin, Teilhard	500
Allen, James	505	Dilgo Khyentse Rinpoche	575
Augustine, Saint	550	Dionysius, the Areopagite	490
Aurobindo, Sri	605	Dogen	740
Bertalanffy, Ludwig van	485	Druckchen Rinpoche	495
Besant, Annie	530	Dzogchen Rinpoche	510
Black Elk, Wallace	499	Eckhart, Meister	705
Bodhidharma	795	Erasmus	500
Bohm, Jakob	500	Fillmore, Charles	515
Bucke, Richard M.	505	Fillmore, Myrtle	505
Buddhananda, Swami	485	Fox, Emmett	470
Butterworth, Eric	495	Gaden Shartse	470
Calvin, John	580	Gandhi, Mahatma	760
Chandra, Ram	540	Gangaji	475
Confucius	590	Goldsmith, Joel	480

Gupta, Mahendranath	505	Patrick, Saint	590
Gyalpo, Lamchen Rinpoche	460	Paul, Pope John II	570
Hall, G. Manley	485	Phuntsok, Khempo	510
Holmes, Ernest	485	Pio, Father	585
Hopkins, Emma Curtis	485	Plotinus	730
Huang, Chungliang Al	485	Po, Huang	960
Huxley, Aldous	485	Poonjai-Ji	520
John, Saint, of the Cross	605	Powell, Robert	525
Karmapa	630	Prabhavananda, Swami	550
Kasyapa	695	Prejnehpad, Swami	505
Khantsa, Jamyung	495	Pulku, Gantey Rinpoche	499
Kline, Jean	510	Ramakrishna	620
Krishna, Gopi	545	Ramdas, Swami	570
Lawrence, Brother	575	Ramanuja Charya, Sri	530
Leadbeater, C. W.	485	Rumi	550
Linpa, Kusum	475	Sai Baba, Shirdi (not	
Luther, Martin	580	Sathya)	485
Madhva Charya, Sri	520	Sannella, Lee	505
Magdeburg, Mechthild von	640	Satchidananda, Swami	605
Maharaj, Nisargadatta	720	Shankara (Sankara Charya)	710
Maharshi, Ramana	720	Smith, Joseph	510
Maezumi, Hakuyu Taizan	505	Socrates	540
Merton, Thomas	515	Steiner, Rudolf	475
Moses de Leon of Granada,		Suzuki, Master Roshi	565
Rabbi	720	Swedenborg, Emanuel	480
Mukerjee, Radhakamal	475	Tagore, Rabindranath	475
Muktananda	655	Tauler, Johann	640
Munroe, Robert	485	Teresa, Mother	710
Nanak	495	Teresa, Saint, of Avila	715
Naranjo, Claudio	465	Tillich, Paul	480
Nityananda, Bhagavan	500	Tzu, Chuang	595
Origen	515	Tzu, Lao	610
Otto, Rudolph	485	Underhill, Evelyn	460
Padmasambhava	595	Vivekananda	610
Pak Chung-Bih, Sotaesan	510	Watts, Alan	485
Palmo, Tenzin	510	White Brotherhood	560
Paramahansa, Yogananda	540	White Plum Asanga	505
Patanjali	715	Yukteswar, Sri	535

Scriptures and Spiritual Writing

Abhinavagupta (Kashmir Shaivinism)	655
A Course in Miracles (workbook)	600
A Course in Miracles (textbook)	550
Aggadah	645
Apocrypha	400
Bodhidharma Zen Teachings	795
Bhagavad-Gita	910
Book of Kells	570
Book of Mormon	405
Cloud of Unknowing	705
Dead Sea Scrolls	260
Dhammapada	840
Diamond Sutra	700
Doctrine and Covenants: Pearl of Great Price	455
Genesis (Lamsa Bible)	660
Gnostic Gospels	400
Gospel of St. Luke	699
Gospel of St. Thomas	660
Granth Sahib (Adi Granth - Sikhs)	505
Heart Sutra	780
Kabbalah	605
King James Bible (from the Greek)	475
Koran	700
Lamsa Bible (from the Aramaic)	495
Lamsa Bible (minus the Old Testament and Book of Revelation, but including Genesis, Psalms, and Proverbs)	880
Lao Tsu: Teachings	610
Lotus Sutra	780
Midrath	665
Mishneh	665
New Testament (King James Version after deletion of the Book of Revelation)	790
New Testament (King Jamess Version from the Greek)	640
Nicene Creed	895
Psalms (Lamsa Bible)	650
Proverbs (Lamsa Bible)	350
Po, Huang, Zen teachings	850
Ramayana	810
Rubaiyat of Omar Khayyam, The	590
Rig Veda	705
Talmud	595
Tibetan Book of the Dead	575
Torah	550
Trinity (concept)	945
Upanishads	970
Vedanta	595
Vedas	970
Vijnana Bhairava	635
Yoga Sutras, Patanjali	740
Zohar	905

Note: The Zen teachings of Huang Po calibrate at 850. Later in life, he continued to evolve to level 960.)

CHAPTER 12

The Devotee

Introduction

Some students are, so to speak, born to spiritual propensity and show an early attraction to religion and spirituality, as well as aesthetics. Some may evidence religiosity or even scrupulosity, with its obsessive fear of sin and compliance with religious dictums. The religiously inclined may also be attracted to becoming clergy or joining holy orders or monastic groups that may emphasize asceticism, service, and voluntary poverty. Such youths often appear to be introspective, serious, and preoccupied with philosophical, moral, and ethical issues.

In contrast, other eventual seekers show a progressive interest in spirituality as they mature and seek answers to the inherent paradoxes and dilemmas of the human condition and their philosophical implications. Commonly, there is contemplation of the traditional existential questions, i.e., Whence did we arise? Where does one go? How 'real' is the 'reality' of God, or is it just a belief system? and the like.

The introspective persons tend to examine these issues early in life, while the extroverts, although perhaps religious, tend to put off these essential questions until a later age or as a consequence of personal life tragedies or catastrophes. 'Hitting bottom' may precipitate sudden conversion experiences in many ordinary people and is a well-known phenomenon in twelve-step and other faith-based groups. Sudden, unexpected calamities, such as a heart attack or the death of someone close, rather frequently precipitate deep spiritual inquiry and self-examination. Of these catastrophes, the near-death experience is the most impressive and intrinsically transformative, for even a brief experience of the Presence turns one's life upside down. A near-death experience also is characterized by the complete loss of the fear of death.

The response of the average rational person, when confronted by the inevitability of death, is to become more seriously committed to religious, moral, and ethical values. For most people, faith and belief in salvation and redemption to compensate for human limitations and frailties are sought through traditional religion. Thus, throughout time, the Divine Teacher (Avatar) is accepted and worshipped as one's eventual advocate or intercessor as Savior by whatever name, such as Jesus Christ, Buddha, Krishna, Muhammad, or of the Hindu pantheon as expressions of Divinity.

All the above are inclusive of faith in Divine Mercy, Grace, Compassion, and ultimate deliverance from the inherent limitations of being human. By self-honesty and spiritual integrity, the inner validity of religion appeals to the rational person. Acceptance of religious truth is confirmed by equanimity in the face of the acceptance of physical death.

A religiously integrous lifestyle is satisfying and results in healthy self-esteem as well as respect for others. Traditional religion provides dependable, practical morality and a set of ethics and guidelines for behavior, values, and character formation.

The diehard skeptic might ask, "But what if God and religion are not true or real?" The answer, of course, is that then they will have lived a good life of virtue for its own reward. Research indicates that religious persons and families show major benefits in every aspect of life, such as health, happiness, longevity, classroom behavior, school grades, social success, and their immune system (Keller, 2004).

As a practical guide in today's world of advanced awareness of the levels of consciousness, a useful rule is to simply avoid sin (anything that calibrates below 200). The validity of spiritual and religious realities is reflected extensively in *Truth vs. Falsehood*, where it can be seen that even just a brief review of the charts of the distribution of the levels of consciousness validates truth in a clear and obvious manner.

Formal traditional religion suffices for the spiritual needs of the vast majority of mankind. In America, approximately ninety percent of the people admittedly believe in God, although a much lower percentage is formally religious. There is, however, a growing segment of the population that is admittedly spiritual and embraces the practice of spiritual values in daily life without the necessity of formal religion per se. As a subpopulation, they have been recently designated as "cultural creatives" (Anderson and Ray, 2000). Many adherents to the tenets of the cultural creatives are friendly to religion but at the same time may keep a formal distance because they see it as too sectarian, restrictive, or divisive. Spiritually-oriented people tend to become familiar with the tenets of a variety of religions and seek to identify the inherent truth that is essential to each. Thus, the most common search in today's world is for universal, practical spiritual principles that are self-evident, have intrinsic value, and do not depend solely on ecclesiastical authority or dogma. To be kind, supportive, and compassionate to all of life is a common, overall prevailing attitude.

Committed spiritual students are thus derived from a variety of sources, including even former atheists and secularists who have undergone an inner transformation as a result of calamity, maturation, or fortuitous circumstances. It is said that there are ten thousand pathways to God, and of these, the pathway of the committed spiritual devotee is traditional and well trodden. The energizing of the serious spiritual commitment is by virtue of the evolution of consciousness, with its concomitant karmic proclivities.

Classically, the readiness for serious spiritual work is referred to as 'ripeness', at which point even hearing a single word, phrase, or name may trigger sudden decision and commitment. The advent of spiritual dedication may thus be subtle, slow, and gradual, and then take a very sudden and major jump. By whatever route, once the seed falls on ready ground, the journey begins in earnest. Commonly, the turning point can be triggered by an unexpected flash of insight, and from that moment on, life changes (as described in Gladwell's *The Tipping Point*, 2002).

The Spiritual Aspirant/Student/'Chela'/Devotee/Seeker

The spiritually inspired tend to become self-educative, searching through spiritual libraries, attending lectures, and visiting various spiritual groups. This is a period of research and exploration of the various avenues and spiritual pathways, as well as belief systems.

For convenience, the calibrated levels of various spiritual practices, pathways, groups, and literature can be ascertained by the consciousness calibration charts in Chapter 11. Among the various religions, it is to be noted that the highest teachings emanate from the evolved teachers themselves, often termed 'mystics', who have transcended the dualistic limitations inherent in ecclesiastical traditions. The core of truth is the pristine, nonlinear essence, which is nondualistic and arises at consciousness level 600. Very rarely, it may evolve still further to transcend the dualities that are intrinsic to even very advanced levels of consciousness. The conscientious devotee accepts as provisional the innate authority of advanced levels of truth, especially if they are corroborated by consciousness calibration.

Notable is that pure spirituality has no requirements, obligations, dependencies, attachments, neediness, or other evidence of specialness, nor the imposition of control, such as signing up members for classes or 'trainings'. Commitment is to the core of truth itself and is free of seduction by proselytization or secrecies. All that is necessary are a curiosity and attraction to truth, which is complete, total, and self-sufficient.

The teachers, teachings, or groups that are found to be attractive or meaningful depend on the stage of evolution of the seeker's level of consciousness at any given time. While the calibrated consciousness level of the typical human advances an average of about five to ten points in a lifetime, in the spiritual seeker, that rate advances much more rapidly and may take very sudden and major leaps. Therefore, this potentiality and likely eventuality should be prepared for in advance.

The Evolutionary Journey

For the serious student, spiritual commitment changes the context of life, which is then viewed from a different perspective. What was once attractive and exciting may now seem superficial, shallow, irrelevant, or even annoying; and what was previously considered to be boring is now attractive and valued as a great opportunity. Preferences and values change, and one may also be surprised at the strength of spiritual energies that, when activated, can be experienced as though one has stepped into a current that is more powerful than one had suspected. Efforts to control and rationally regulate the process are progressively revealed to be illusory. On the other hand, some trends that seem simple on the surface may turn out to be resistant and tenacious. Those that at first glance appear almost impossible may be resolved with surprisingly relative ease.

It will be discovered that all experiences and phenomena have an intrinsic value to spiritual evolution and discovery. Eventually, it becomes necessary to simply subordinate the personal will to the process itself, which tends to become progressively stronger. The unfolding of the life of the serious spiritual devotee becomes increasingly orchestrated by the Self rather than the ego/self. Former presumptions become meaningless, and Divine Intelligence and awareness reinterpret meanings that were once considered beyond comprehension. Thereby does the world continuously become 'newly born' each instant, as by the radiance of the Self, the clouds of illusion fade away and Essence replaces appearance.

Operational Values and Principles

Along the spiritual pathway blocks and temptations appear, as well as doubts and fears. Classically, they have been termed the 'tests' that arise from the ego that does not relish relinquishment of dominion. These are overcome by reaffirmation of goals and commitment, as well as by reinforcing counterbalancing principles, such as dedication, tenacity, constancy, courage, conviction, and intention. The greater the challenge, the greater is the development of inner strength, decision, and determination. By persistence and discipline, it can be seen that temptations are options to merely refuse rather than call for attack or negation. This is also a consequence of the subordination of the lesser to the greater, and thus, priority prevails by an act of the will, assisted by surrendering the personal will to God.

All the above are subsumed under the quality of devotion, which is empowered by love and not just reason or mental comprehension. Devotion is of the heart for, at times, it is solely by the power of the heart and Divine Love that an obstacle can be transcended.

A useful practice is to look ahead on the spiritual road and see what will eventually have to be surrendered, such as attachments to the world and its values. This awareness facilitates greater ease, willingness, and readiness to surrender the attachments voluntarily. (If not now, when?) The 'letting go' of materialism and worldly gain is facilitated by the realization that everything belongs to God, and that humans have only temporary custody or stewardship. Thus, in reality, there is no 'my' anything. In fact, nobody even 'owns' their own body, for it belongs to the world and returns to the world from whence it came. As a paradox, it will be noted that the ego/self believes that it has ownership of its possessions and properties but, upon examination, the opposite is true, that is, one is owned by their possessions and properties, not the reverse.

The capabilities that ensue from spiritual devotion

and commitment are often of greater magnitude than originally suspected, and the seemingly 'impossible' turns out to be 'possible'. What seems impossible dissolves as such if one imagines whether they could let go of an attachment if a loaded gun were pointed at their head. One can also witness the extremes to which humans have gone over time and in other cultures in the service of devotion, including major deprivation, hardship, and voluntary sacrifice. Although these options may not appear during spiritual practice, their psychological equivalents may well appear to be 'sacrifices'.

It is helpful to remember that value and attraction are in the eye of the beholder and are not qualities of the world itself. What is imagined to be 'out there' stems from 'in here'. The same applies to cherished positionalities and seductive presumptions. There are no temptations 'out there', and their attraction diminishes by simple refusal and renunciation.

Religion versus 'Religionism'

Devotion often starts with dedication to the religion of one's upbringing and is therefore experienced as complete and satisfying. Faith plus worship, prayer, and religious observances serve the needs of the majority of truly religious people. Their faith is often augmented by selfless service or support of humanitarian activities.

The traditional pathway of religion is self-fulfilling and leads to advanced states of consciousness and selfless saintliness that may eventuate as dedication to the goal of Enlightenment itself, which is frequently associated with a change of lifestyle.

The downside trap of religion could best be termed

'religionism', by which overzealousness is expressed as
extremism or by the alternative of worshipping the
religion instead of God. This is characterized by an
almost obsessive-compulsive preoccupation with the
written word and ecclesiastical doctrine. This aberration is typified as 'confusing the map with the territory',
a phrase taken from *Our Language and Our World*
(Hayakawa, 1971) and also expressed as 'missing the
forest for the trees'. This signifies limitation by the intellect
to content and ignorance of context, meaning, and significance, which reflect conversion of language/symbols to
subjective realization and contemplation.

This error results in religionists' using concrete
quotations of religious doctrine to justify behaviors
that are the exact opposite of the true, abstract, nonlinear meaning of the cited scriptures. (The Inquisition;
burning heretics at the stake; Islamic terrorism; religious wars; and hatreds, including prosecution and
genocide, are some examples.) Thus, religionism in the
extreme becomes fanaticism and a pathological,
destructive aberration that often seeks secular totalitar-
ian power and political extremism.

As is well known, it is a simple matter to find a quotation that justifies any position when it is taken out of
context (e.g., confusing the 'sword of Truth' with the
'sword of steel'). Thus, there is a very wide disparity
between dedication and zealotry, and by their fruits,
the distinction becomes obvious. That pathological
states may cloak themselves in religiosity does not
preclude the more serious fact that they are intrinsically
pathological despite the efforts of apologists to ignore
the distinction.

As would be expected, religious zealotry calibrates

extremely low, and, in contrast, true religious devotion calibrates very high. Religious extremism also contributes to the social appeal of secularism and even militant antireligionism, as was seen in the wake of communism (Tibet, China, etc.). True religious devotion is not coercive nor does it impair the lives of others or imperil their survival. Thus, balance counters extremism and is a component of spiritual wisdom and maturation that offsets the substitution of rituals for religious observances. The value of scripture is in its meaning and capacity to facilitate subjective transformation that is often consequent to interpretation of meaning rather than literal translation.

Renunciation As A Process

The primary renunciation is to refuse and refute the value and attraction of that inner theater processor of the ego called the 'experiencer', which is desirous of attention as a focus of energy. The 'experiencer' is a quality of attention processing that greedily and endlessly searches for a subject of focus, interest, and excitement. This aspect of consciousness is like a compulsively exploratory probing fueled by curiosity. It is greedy for linear data, sensation, and form, as well as the payoff of emotionality itself. It feeds on 'change' and something 'happening' and is attracted by the allure of excitement. (Witness the pile-up of slow cars as they pass even a minor accident on any highway.) Its characteristics are also displayed by nature films of the creatures that live at the bottom of or in the sea.

The 'experiencer' consumes energy, and as a result, the human being requires sleep for renewal of energy and the capacity to function. It is this focus of the experiencer that is to be transcended by meditation and contemplation.

The experiencer is hungry for novelty and 'interesting' data about which the ego is eager to react in order to keep the emotional circus activated. The experiencer's circuit is seductive to involvement and participation in the kaleidoscopic melodrama of life.

It is important to appreciate that the reactive, eager 'experiencer' aspect of the ego seeks to be on center stage and performs as the inner 'celebrity' of the self. It is the hero/heroine of the ongoing story that is entitled 'me', 'I', and 'myself' and is thereby considered to be of great value and supposed worth. It is the focus of the self's narcissistic involvement and is thereby highly invested with psychological energy and prioritization. The 'experiencer' is the central actor/actress that is credited as the doer of deeds, the thinker of thoughts, and the secret causal agency of actions and decisions. It is the victor and the victim. Most important of all, it is believed to be the core, source, essence, and cause of one's life and therefore central and crucial to existence itself. Its demise is thus inwardly feared as death and therefore heavily defended. It is this experiencer/personhood that is the substitute identity for the Realty that is the true Self.

Pitfalls and Distractions: Mind and the World

The limitations of the karmically inherited ego/mind result in an innate proclivity to error and are a consequence of both innocence and naïveté. Unaided, it is not able to transcend its innate limitations nor does it even realize the extent of its impairments. Like a computer whose hardware will automatically accept any software input, the human mind is unprotected and vulnerable to almost any conceivable programming to the degree of even the most bizarre and extreme falsity of which the classic 'Luciferic inversion' is a striking and currently displayed example (i.e., to misidentify opposites by which good becomes classified as evil, and vice versa).

The unprotected mind is impressionable, and even the most basic protection of reason can be overruled by emotionality or social programming. The whole world's population has commonly held completely false beliefs for many centuries and still does to this day. Therefore, to depend on popular belief systems is to be prone to error (e.g., Mackay's *Extraordinary Popular Delusions & the Madness of Crowds*, [1841], 2003). All such assumptions should be viewed as provisional at best in view of the inherent limitations of the mind itself.

Other than the irreducible, irrefutable fact that one *is*, all else is presumptive at best. This does not mean, however, that skepticism (cal. 160) is a substitute for wisdom for it also is based on an illusion. Other than the Self and/or an advanced Teacher, the mind has not had, until recently, a verifiable source of assessment of truth.

Due to the evolution of consciousness, a means is now available for not only discerning truth from falsehood but also of calibrating the degree of truth as compared to the Absolute. Therefore, the pragmatic Map of Consciousness is an extremely useful tool for it can throw light where there is darkness to reveal that which is hidden or obscure.

The key to transcending the inherent limitations of

the ego/mind is humility, without which the mind is hopelessly trapped in its illusory house of mirrors. The evolution of the intellect as reason, logic, and science eventuated as the upside of modern civilization with its great benefits to humanity. It is a confirmable observation that the higher the calibration of a thought system, the greater has been the benefit to humanity and the relief of its suffering inherent to ignorance. The overall positive effect of the evolution of consciousness/mind is obvious within the linear dimension, but it becomes even more so as consciousness advances past the linear domain at calibration level 499, when the nonlinear spiritual energy becomes dominant.

The educated spiritual student of today has fortunate advantages that were not available in the past. Sophistication about the nature of the ego/mind and its evolutionary foundations is a distinct advantage for it facilitates self-honesty and awareness that historically was made difficult or even impossible due to programming with guilt and shame that resulted in denial and repression of the awareness of inner hidden proclivities.

Pitfalls and Distractions

An area of limitation that is often overlooked by spiritual students is that of the social programming of belief systems, which is the consequence of memes (presumptive stereotypes via brief slogans and repetitious ideas), as well as more vociferous propaganda and political distortion of the implications of facts. These promulgate via their cleverly concealed seduction to intellectual vanity (Dawkins, 1992; Beck and Cowan, 1996). This downside of vulnerability to rhetoric was also discussed at length in *Truth vs. Falsehood* (Chapter 12).

Like anyone else in society, the mind of the aspirant has also unwittingly been programmed. This often escapes notice unless highlighted by a Teacher. Many students adhere to a stereotype of what 'being spiritual' implies. Thus, there are often political/social/intellectual stereotyped beliefs that need to be investigated as naïve programs.

To seriously seek enlightenment is a very strict discipline that therefore eschews the attraction of involvement in supposed spiritual movements that are actually intrinsically political in nature and factional. The attraction of 'changing the world' (for the presumed better, of course) appeals to the naïve idealism of the inner spiritual adolescent and is transcended with maturity. The nature of human life is the automatic consequence of the overall level of human consciousness itself. Therefore, to benefit the world, it is necessary to change not the world but oneself, for what one becomes is influential by virtue of its essence (nonlinear) and not its actions (limited and linear). The purpose of action is to control others. Force (emotional or otherwise) results in counterforce; power comes from the nonlinear level of consciousness itself.

Straight and narrow is the path, for without inner discipline, the spiritual energy becomes dissipated in diverse attractions. Profound silence is more influential and beneficial than an avalanche of redundant words and actions that emanate from the spiritual ego and its platitudinous rationalizations. Spiritual rhetoric is still just rhetoric and represents spiritual sophistry. Commitment to Enlightenment alters and recontextualizes social roles.

There are many attractive, aberrant spiritual groups, techniques, practices, and teachings that become glamorized, popularized, peddled, and even literally marketed. There is also seduction by proselytization, pop-culture promotional venues, and effusive emotionality (Lewis, 2001). All these attractions signify the seeking of a gain by their promotion. In contrast, that which is integrous is self-fulfilled and therefore does not need promotion.

Eager, naïve students may be impressed by the opinions and enthusiasm of followers of attractive, diversionary spiritual groups and leaders. Some are impressed by web sites, celebrities, or emotional claims. There are supposed 'avatars' by the dozens who are imagined to be the great saviors of humanity (sometimes even by a prescribed date). These routinely calibrate not only low but often below level 200—the critical level of Truth. Often added to the attraction are claims of performance of the miraculous and unnatural oddities. Thus, it is not unusual at all for very famous, highly proclaimed 'miracle workers' to calibrate as low as 175. It is therefore best to avoid the bizarre or the unlikely and to remember that there is no 'person' who performs miracles in a cause-and-effect kind of contextualization. The truly 'miraculous' is the emergence into actuality of potentiality as a consequence of an overall contextual field that includes karma, and it is therefore not 'caused' by nor can it be claimed by an individual personality.

As with any human endeavor, there is a sequence of levels of maturation and mastery to progressive levels of sophistication, education, experience, and acquisition of skills and knowledge. Early in the search for truth, there is vulnerability to the allure of various promulgated programs and personalities that tend to become an attractive theater invitational to mystical and magical allure. There are glib 'masters' who even claim to be 'higher than Jesus' and attract great wealth. Others promote various forms of sexuality and even 'holy sex' encounters with the leader. (These persons all calibrate below 200, although some of them were temporarily in the 500s early in their careers.)

Also invitational is the seductive lure of 'secrets' and membership (at a cost) in 'select' inner subgroups, with accompanying titles and privileges. Common to such groups are also submission and obedience to the leader as well as a variety of personal restrictions. All of these linear distractions denote specialness rather than rational distractions of essence.

Common are claims to exotic 'other dimensions' or realms with unique nominalization. None of the aberrant pathways, teachers, or organizations calibrates at an acceptable level of truth, and none appears in the list of confirmed spiritual teachers or teachings (Chapter 11). The rule 'caveat emptor' obviously applies and is adhered to by the wise (Partridge, 2003).

While exploration of the new may seem like a harmless educative and entertaining novelty, even that degree of exposure has unanticipated consequences that are usually unrecognized. The mind is like the hardware of a computer that is instantly programmable by linear content as well as nonverbal energy patterns. Thus, the explorer of the pop pseudospirituality of the astral circus of the typical 'New Age Fair' inadvertently picks up a variety of energies that are out of awareness.

The best protection is avoidance out of humble respect for the limitations and the weaknesses of the ego/mind. To flirt with that which is seemingly harmless is attractive to negative subliminal energy patterns. The acquired spiritual flaws may later affect the student adversely in ways that are out of awareness but detectable by others. Thus, avoidance of that which can be deleterious to or delay spiritual evolution is advised out of humility and respect for limitations rather than fear. As mentioned elsewhere, traditional scripture advises to eschew the paranormal and just 'don't go there'.

As with other attractions, it is the 'experiencer' aspect of the ego that leads to involvement with distractions and naïve errors of judgment, mistaken decisions, or conclusions. The avoidance of diversions and attractions is not based on judgmentalism but instead on respecting the value of the validation of truth. There are numerous integrous teachers and teachings; thus, it is not necessary to seek for novel byways. The great traditional pathways have sufficed for thousands of years, and their essential truths have been confirmed by experience. They are now even more adequately understood and confirmable.

Frequently, serious spiritual students become waylaid by attractive, deviant pathways, schools, and teachings and thereby devote time and energy in fruitless pursuit of spiritual illusions. This may take up years, decades, or even whole lifetimes that sometimes end up in regret or even bitter disappointment. With the current availability of the techniques of calibrating levels of truth, such errors can be circumvented. There are even professional 'deprogrammers' to assist in recovery from cult indoctrination and brainwashing that can result in severe loss of reality testing and rationality, even to the degree of cult group suicide or bombing the innocent, allegedly 'for God'.

Alignment with a Pathway

Chapter 11 gives the necessary information and guidelines to ascertain purity, authenticity, and validity of teachers, traditions, religions, spiritual schools, and organizations. Dedication is a more important sign of integrity than enthusiasm. It is necessary to have faith in a pathway and clear away doubts to ascertain if they are realistic or merely forms of resistance. A seeker should have the security and support of inner certainty and firm conviction that are consequent to study, personal research, and investigation. Thus, a pathway should be intrinsically reconfirming by discovery and inner experience. A true pathway unfolds, is self-revelatory, and is subject to reconfirmation experientially.

As spiritual awareness advances, the flow of spiritual energy increases and enables transcending prior, seemingly insurmountable, obstacles. As the attractions of the world and emotions decrease, there is a progressive attraction to qualities, such as beauty, lovability, and peace, rather than things or seeming gains. Forgiveness becomes a habitual attitude, and the innate innocence of all Creation shines forth. The teachings of great saints and teachers become one's own from within.

Q: Please discuss materialism.

A: Formally, the term denotes belief in the theory that the material/physical world is the only reality and that all phenomena are the consequence of and can be explained in terms of physicality. It is expressed as physical reductionism in the traditional scientific Newtonian paradigm and in intellectual discourses pertaining to the arguments of 'bottom up' versus 'top down' theories of causality. The subject recurs in conferences pertaining specifically to 'science and consciousness', or science and religion or theology.

Although the subject may sound abstract and primarily philosophical, in practice it has profound practical consequences. Dialectical materialism emerged as Marxism, which fomented worldwide revolution and the deaths of many millions of people. Materialism denies the reality of Divinity as the Source of Creation and life, and consequently, it calibrates (as does Marx) at 130. Mechanistic materialism sources skepticism (cal. 160), which is limited to the linear domain. It denies the reality of the nonlinear, which calibrates at level 500 or above. Paradoxically, although skepticism ridicules faith, it has great faith in its own very limited paradigm and philosophical presumptions of which it is naïvely unaware.

When applied to consciousness research, the bottom-up theorists attempt to demonstrate that consciousness is solely the product of neuronal activity. All such projects calibrate very low and fail to demonstrate the materialistic premise. The last research project of Crick (of DNA fame) before he died was so designed (it calibrated at 150-160). Thus, the design of all similar projects calibrates very low and reflects not only a fallacious basis and defect of vision but also a philosophical, antispiritual, or atheistic bias. Therefore, such research is also not truly scientific to begin with and violates the principles of objective, unbiased, pristine investigation.

In the field of spiritual endeavor, materialism denotes an ego attachment to linear limitation and an imbalance of projected worth to that which is transitory at the expense of spiritual values that are long term. It is the consequence of 'left-brain only' processing of information that precludes awareness of abstract meaning and inference. Thus, it reflects impairment of potentiality, which is consequent to brain physiology itself (see Brain Function chart in Chapter 6). The alternate error is to give a negative connotation to all interest in that which is 'worldly', such as money or possessions that can be respected as assets, which requires stewardship and responsibility.

Because human existence includes the physicality of the body and its requirements, the material world is appropriately important and represents Creation in linear form. Thus, a balanced view is to accept and integrate materiality from an overall spiritual viewpoint and appreciate but not become attached to that which is transitory. 'Wearing the world like a light garment' expresses an attitude of appropriate balance.

Asceticism may have a value in the attempt to overcome sensory attachment, but extremes may also signify fear or aversion. The 'lure' of the world is not innate to the world but instead is a projection of desire by the ego that ascribes inflated value to that which is linear and transitory.

Q: Can the world thus be designated as 'secular'?
A: That can be a limiting positionality reflective of contextualization. True secularism is the belief that

denies the reality of the presence of the nonlinear within the linear. Secularism (cal. 165) ignores or denies the Reality of Divinity as the source of existence and Creation.

Q: How best to choose a pathway?
A: The selection is a consequence of what a person has become and where they are in the evolution of consciousness. Personal choice is the result of myriad factors, such as family of origin, culture, education, age, karmic patterns, personal relationships, and life experiences. In addition, it is now possible to ascertain the level of truth of various teachings and organizations so that the spiritual student of today has additional advantages. A higher calibration does not mean 'better than' but instead delineates the level of an expression of Reality and spiritual truth.

The most important principles are those that are most basic, such as good will, forgiveness, respect, integrity, lovingness, and compassion. The blocks to these are relatively easy to discern and resolve with recontextualization, which reduces or removes positionalities. An adequate pathway is one that offers the means of resolving conflicts rather than compounding them with categorization as 'right' or 'wrong'. Hate, greed, etc., are 'wrong', of course, but that is not of any help in resolving them. An effective pathway should offer other ways of seeing things so that obstacles dissolve by a mere comprehensive understanding. This means the identification of the obstructive positionality and clarifying the duality that is the basis of the conflict.

Q: Can you give an example?

A: Each positionality is the result of a construct, like building blocks. It is unraveled by inner investigation. A seeming problem requires honest research. Let us use 'hate' as an example. What is its basis in a given situation? Envy? Jealousy? Fear? Pride? It is usually due to a combination of factors. Is it rivalry for status? Competition? Hurt feelings? An insult to the prideful-ness of the ego? Being right? Winning? Threat? Programmed by propaganda/media?

Completely resolving even one issue tends to decrease all of them, for at the bottom is usually the narcissistic ego's problem of humility, which is the keystone to surrender. The central conflicts to each level were examined in some detail in *Transcending the Levels of Consciousness*, but essentially, they are similar. Each positionality is held in place by a dualistic set of attractions and their corresponding aversions. With humility arises the acceptance that everyone is somewhere along the evolution of consciousness, and spiritual development for that is the core pur-pose of human life in this world.

Q: Why does life in the world seem to be so difficult at times?

A: Multiple evolutionary species coexist on a planet that itself goes through constant change. Hominids are of recent origin, and Homo sapiens are a mix-ture of great variation in levels of consciousness, not only of individuals but also whole cultures and countries. Still present are illiterate stone-age and nomadic tribal cultures along with sophisti-cated, highly-educated, computerized countries with very advanced technology and economies.

In addition, there are different, often conflicting religions and antireligious belief systems as well as their political ideologies. On top of the difficulties of all these potentially conflicting diversities is the primordial, inherent basic obstacle that the human mind is, by its very design, unable to discern truth from falsehood. In all recorded human history, peace has prevailed only seven percent of the time and war ninety-three percent of the time. The linear dimension entails suffering; thus, the best Teachers of history taught the ways to Salvation or Enlightenment as the only answer to escape from that suffering.

CHAPTER 13

Transcending Identification with the Ego/Self

Introduction

This subject is the core of all spiritual endeavors. The undoing of the identification with the ego/self is the primary focus of spiritual evolution and is the enigma that has baffled even the most erudite minds of history. The crux of the problem is misidentification with qualities of the ego/mind processing function already identified with the linearity of the localization of phenomena. This is a natural consequence associated with the physical reality of the experience of life as a body. The primary problem is misidentification of the actual source of subjectivity and the presumption that it is local rather than nonlocal.

An analogy to the above would be that of electricity, which is a generic type of energy and therefore 'impersonal'. When it runs through a toaster or a fan, the device would then mistakenly identify itself as being the primary source and not realize that it is only an outlet unit. Without the 'life' energy of electricity, each receiving unit would be inert.

The disassembly of the ego mechanism is facilitated by an understanding of its evolutionary origins and progression over eons of time, which have already been alluded to with charts and examples. By historical origin, the requirement for the survival of life in physically separate units required acquisition and therefore the capacity for investigative processing of energy sources. This processing function then became identified as 'I' by virtue of experiential subjectivity. To continue the analogy, the primordial source of life energy is independent of localization as units. The units assume themselves to be primary rather than merely expressions of a universality. The energy of life is a radiance from the field of consciousness, which is the mode of the Presence of Divinity that manifests in physicality as Creation. The capacity for Enlightenment is merely a consequence of consciousness returning to its source, which is Divinity Immanent as Self.

The ego/self identifies with its various functions and qualities and labels them by ownership as 'me' and says that is 'who I am'. This results in the vanity of authorship, an error that originated during evolution as a consequence of identification with the experience of the senses. Thus comes about a typical conclusion that 'I' itch instead of 'the body' itches. The same error of authorship/ownership occurs with feelings and thoughts in that the witness identifies with the subject and the content of the experiencer.

The experiencer function is an information probe that collects linear data and therefore is an 'it' and not a 'me'. It is a functional processing unit similar to the senses of smell or touch. Thus, the Buddha spoke of man as having six senses instead of five and contextualized the brain as a sensory organ of sensation, perception, and information processing.

Prior to the evolution of consciousness reaching calibration level 200, there is no innate subjective awareness of beingness or existence as such. The living organisms experience the qualities of their existence without realizing the reality of existence, is-ness or beingness. Although it 'is', it is not innately conscious and substitutes experiencing in lieu of the awareness of existence. As consciousness continues to evolve, the quality and the value of existence itself arise, and hence the search for its source.

Disassembly of the Ego/Self

Once the evolutionary structure and function of the ego are understood, its disassembly is facilitated by the inner decision to pursue that which is real and eternal rather than that which is temporal, transitory, and ephemeral.

When one has chosen the spiritual pathway, the question arises of how to proceed through ordinary human life now that one has a different overall motivation. It will be found that, as a consequence, it is not usually necessary to initially abandon ordinary life but instead to recontextualize it. Curiously, the degree to which one values one's own life determines the answer. Those who see it as a precious gift do not wish to waste it on that which is trivial and transitory, for the demise of the physical body is an inevitable certainty. The pleasures of life can be accepted as a gift while rejecting becoming attached to them. In the past, especially during the era of Gothic religionism, piety was equated with penance, guilt, poverty, sackcloth, and ashes. A more effective form of renunciation is to relinquish the projection of value onto the world and its overvaluation. Worldly success still occurs but is accepted with gratitude instead of pride, and humility allows continuation in the world without egoistic perceptual projections.

Rejecting the seduction of the activities of the mind and its endless operations is the most effective and ultimate renunciation. Upon even casual observation, one sees that it is composed of an endless kaleidoscope of opinions, viewpoints, attitudes, preconclusions, assumptions, and prevailing social positionalities popularized by the media and glamorized by acclaim. Thus, the inner process is primarily one of de-energizing illusions rather than one of acquiring new information. Awareness is predominately revealing in nature rather than a private acquisition. The Self is already aware of Reality and does not need to learn more about it.

'Divine ignorance' is a classic term that denotes the wisdom of humility. The mind, in and of itself, cannot discern appearance from essence, and thus the devotee learns to turn a deaf ear to thinkingness and focuses instead on the knowingness of wisdom from within, as revealed by the great teachers over long periods of history and reaffirmed as the Presence of Self. These teachers, even though widely separated over the centuries by time and geography, are in mutual agreement. Formal religions always calibrate at a level below the truth of the teachings of their founders. Most spiritual students therefore seek confirmation of the essence of truth within each, which is different from 'syncretism', the assumption that all religions are equally true. Because there are major errors in all classical religions, syncretism (although it sounds attractive) would also include the errors of all the existent religions and their variations of translation.

A problem with using the mind to discover truth is that it often cannot tell the forest from the trees and instead focuses on problematic irrelevancies and extraneous diversions, such as, Did the Buddha 'really' sit under a bodi tree? Or, Where did Jesus spend his lost years? Did the Red Sea actually part? Is the crucial, eternal truth that would save mankind lost somewhere in a cave? Will the world end in 2068? Are the 'end times' here? Are UFO messengers here to save us? The ego loves to fiddle with hypothetical conundrums and thus extends its attraction via fallacious pursuits. If they were of great value, they would have been mentioned by Jesus, Buddha, Krishna, or the great sages over the many centuries.

The errors of specific content can be bypassed by aligning with primordial, inviolate spiritual principles that would avoid postulations as to whether God is angry, or whether wearing a beard or a hat is of any importance. The ego is eventually cancelled out by the Truth of the Self, and not by religious contention. The content of religious observances is of secondary importance compared to the intention because intention is independent of circumstances and irrelevant details.

Study, concentration, and attention tend to narrow focus and emphasize content and details, whereas contemplation is aligned with the overall field and its contextualization of significance, meaning, and value. The ego loves detail and linear labeling. It likes stances such as, Isn't that awful? and has endless questions like, How come? Conflict is therefore of the ego, and harmony is of the spirit. The personal ego/self never runs out of drama and problems, which are invented as a tool of self-propagation. In its own defense, the ego manufactures 'boredom' if precluded from excitement, but it still manages to remain center stage by wailing like a two-year-old who is not being entertained. To reveal the game of the ego, it is only necessary when one is bored to merely ask, Why am I bored? This leads to self-inquiry, which reveals the role of what has been termed the 'experiencer'.

Self-Inquiry as a Spiritual Technique

This was a favorite teaching of Ramana Maharshi who recommended posing the question, "Who am I?" the purpose of which was to direct attention from the experiencer to the Source of Awareness itself, and thus lead from the self to the Self. Taken out of context, the famous quote, "Who am I?" may, however, lead most often to exploration of identity content or definition rather than to intuiting context. It might be more beneficial to ask, What am I? 'What' is impersonal and aligned with the universal energy, while 'Who' is aligned with the personal and the linear.

The Pace of Worldly Life

Devotional commitment to inner spiritual work is not usually a major interference early in the process but may later even necessitate a change of occupation and relationships. Adjustments enable ordinary life to go on up to a certain point, at which time there is a loss of interest in linear processing and externalization of goals.

Spiritual work eventually takes on a predominant priority that often results in major changes. Frequently, the spiritual drive gains momentum and becomes the predominant focus in what could be called the 'radical stage'. Although it seems to be a drivenness, it is actually the consequence of the attraction of the Self that is now energizing the endeavor. One is not propelled by the past but magnetically attracted by the future. The Self acts like gravity that becomes ever more powerful as one nears its center. The effect of Self is akin also to a magnetic attraction whose effect increases as one nears the goal. The passion for Divinity results in a de-energizing interest in worldliness since the Self has no needs, wants, or desires, even for the body itself.

In more advanced stages, leaving the world is a common phenomenon. For one thing, the ego then has 'nothing to do' and is put into retirement. Subsequent capacity for activity is problematic and reflects residual karmic propensities. At very advanced levels above 600, the option to leave the physicality appears, and the majority of those who reach that level do so. Thus, statistically, at any one time, there are only a few very advanced sages on the planet by virtue of having transcended the innate evolutionary purpose of human life. Rarer still is it for an enlightened sage to return to and interact with the world, which requires the activation of an aspect of consciousness that could be called the 'persona'. This is essentially and functionally only a quality of communication. There is no 'self' that communicates, and the communication is its own self-sufficient reality. Thus, the communication has no 'purpose' but merely emanates as a quality of its own essence. 'Personhood' is a projection of the observer and not a quality of the teacher.

Q: The description and analysis of the core of spiritual endeavor clarifies the spiritual process that has often been clouded by mystification and obscure religiosity.

A: The true devotee welcomes clarity and precision. The naïve seeker is often enamored by religiosity and mystification. Ceremonial practices and trappings can have an attractive glamour by which spirituality becomes romanticized with a mystical, magical, or even theatrical allure. Some practices lead to trance states or altered states of consciousness. The impressionable seeker is attracted by unusual phenomena that are actually irrelevant, such as the siddhis. In contrast, the real core of spiritual endeavor sounds mundane and unexciting.

Q: If the ego has developed and dominated life for multimillions of years and continues to dominate human life, can such a strong proclivity actually be transcended?

A: The ego is not the actual reality or source of life or existence and is therefore vulnerable to dissolution. It is primordial but not essentially sovereign. It is dominant only until its illusory quality is recognized. Until de-energnized, it edits perception. To merely recognize that it is not the actual substrate of reality but only an evanescent appearance already begins to reduce its influence.

Q: Please further clarify the comments on Ramana Maharshi's method of 'self-inquiry'.

A: The method is worded as "Who am I?" The term 'who' suggests a linear definition or even a recontextualization of personal identity. Basically, the question is correct, for if properly understood, it leads from identification with the personal self to the universal Self. What gives the sense of 'I' its subjective quality of reality is the radiance of the true Self, which is the Source of the Reality that emanates as the Presence. To clarify the pursuit, it is helpful to search for the innate quality that accords the subjective experiential sense of identity itself. It may be more fruitful to search for the source of the quality of subjectivity, which is not a 'who' but an innate quality of sentient life.

Q: That is focusing on 'what' rather than on 'who' is searching for the truth?

A: Yes. It will lead to the discovery that there is no 'who' that is searching but some innate quality itself. The real Self brings up the false self for investigation, which eventually leads to the disassembly of the ego structure itself. In the beginning, a seeker assumes there is a personal self that is seeking the real Self. Actually, it is the real Self that is drawing the seeker to it.

Q: The pursuit of Enlightenment appears to be a very major decision with possible major impact on ordinary lifestyles.

A: This may seem to be a source of worry or anxiety when it is first heard. In due time, resolution occurs as a consequence of recontextualization and a shift in values. What may be perceived as disruptive by the ego at calibrated levels below 600 is not experienced as such at 600 or over when relinquishment of worldly life is natural and welcomed as a relief.

The Self manages the transition. Most questions about adjustments or seeming sacrifices do not take into consideration the power of decision itself, which increases in intensity as the barriers are removed. Devotion dissolves fear, doubt, and hesitation and clarifies uncertainty. Intention also becomes ever stronger as does trust in God. Then arises the inner decision to totally abandon oneself to God.

The evolutionary pathway is self-reinforcing and self-confirming as it progresses. The 'you' that anticipates the future now is not the same 'you' that will have to later adjust to very different conditions. Identification shifts from the content of personal self to the contextual field of transcendent Self. What is seemingly impossible to the self is easy and simple to the Self.

Q: **All doubts and questions arise from the ego's perceptions and projected values.**

A: That is true. Therefore, all anticipations and projections into the hypothetical future are illusory because the Self that emerges becomes progressively dominant and is free of worldly attachments or projected values. It has no 'needs' to worry about and is autonomous and sufficient unto itself. It has no 'wants' that need to be sacrificed so none are necessary. A butterfly no longer needs a cocoon.

Q: **That is reassuring.**

A: Divinity is Infinite Love. Within its Presence, even relinquishment of bodily existence is not a 'problem' or even a source of resistance. If it serves Divine Providence, physicality walks on to fulfill its karmic destiny and commitment. If, on the other hand, it just falls over and quits breathing, that is just fine also. As the ego dissolves, so do all its fears and presumptions. The Inner Reality is immune to considerations or doubts. The Self is Certainty.

Q: **Despite dedication to the goal of Enlightenment, the mind seems reluctant, resistant, or even**

too lazy to go through the necessary process. How can that be overcome?

A: Resistance is to be expected and accepted as an innate quality of the ego. Part of its function is stabilization in order to facilitate performance and reliability. It does not like to feel out of control or off balance and is thus resistant to being questioned or examined, which is perceived as a potential threat to its sovereignty.

The ego has a vested interest in its positionalities, presumptions, and assumptions. There is therefore an ambivalence regarding change—on the one hand, it is exciting and interesting, but on the other hand, it can be viewed as an unwelcome challenge and resented. Thus, it tends to maintain the status quo, even if doing so continues to be unsatisfactory, for example, repeating the same resistances over and over, hoping for a different outcome.

Q: Is inertia characteristic of the ordinary ego?

A: *Tamas* is the guna (energy) of resistance that is overcome by rajas, the energy of activity and effort. *Rajas* is the response to motivation and dedication to actually reach *Sattwa*, the state of peace and tranquility. Tamas is reinforced by the resistances of fear or guilt at the prospect of self-inquiry.

Q: How can the underlying fears of guilt or shame be overcome?

A: It is necessary to hold in mind during all inner investigation (as well as in the perception of others) that the ego/mind is in the process of evolution and is innately innocent by virtue of its

evolutionary structure. It cannot discern appearance from essence. Therefore, compassion for self
and others is a requisite for major transformation
and spiritual growth.

Dominance by instinctual motivations is diminished by simple acceptance rather than guilt or
condemnation, that is, 'of course' the ego is selfish,
greedy, vain, and resentful. That is to be expected.
But now, such attitudes can be seen as no longer
serviceable or productive. Compassion for all of life
includes one's own as well. Old habitual styles of
perception and thinking diminish when no longer
valued or seen as essential to survival or success.
Many strong habitual motivations recede merely as
a consequence of recontextualization.

**Q: How does one overcome the apprehension
about 'bad feelings' arising consequent to
looking within oneself?**

A: Decide that all 'bad' feelings are fallacious and faulty
habits of the mind. Respect for self and others then
replaces guilt or fear. The ego is unaware of the
gifts of the spirit that more than compensate for the
surrender or 'loss' of ego positions. These gifts are
often subtle, such as an increase in self-esteem and
reduction in one's overall anxiety level.

Q: Can you provide a concrete example?

A: The ego thinks success is due to drive and ambition
plus prideful competition, cutting corners, taking
advantage of others, etc. It is not aware that people
who are earnest, honest, integrous, and dedicated
are highly prized and adequately rewarded by

society. These are rewards by invitation and not just zealous acquisition. Excellence itself is self-rewarding and brings gratification that is not dependent on externals. The reward that is often overlooked is the increase in inner strength, courage, and fortitude that results in greater inner security and self-confidence.

Q: But in daily life, temptations abound. Are they not to be refused or resisted?

A: Temptation, seduction, desirability, and allure are all projections having to do with appearance and presumptions. These are associated with programmed fantasies of gain. Satisfaction of projected values constitutes the world of illusion. Happiness itself is directly correlated with the overall level of consciousness rather than with any external factors. External factors are vulnerable and have to be fearfully guarded; in contrast, inner values are self-reinforcing and immune to turmoil or circumstances. This is a common realization among survivors of major catastrophes.

Q: Spiritual work sometimes appears to involve anticipation of loss.

A: Loss is a presumption based on the ego's perceptions and projected values. In general, the ego's loss is illusory and instead constitutes a gain to the Self. All ego positions represent vulnerability. Their surrender results in greater inner security and pleasure in life. Eventually, one analogously feels 'bullet-proof' and independent of external circumstances. Even the survival of the body itself eventually becomes irrelevant for its transitoriness is accepted.

Q: But is not survival itself due to the ego's motives and mechanisms?

A: That is also an illusion. Survival is a consequence of the Self, not the self. It is only because of the Self that the ego is of service for a prescribed period of earthly time. When the ego/mind is silenced, life goes on autonomously, paradoxically even seeing effort as effortless. All comes about as a consequence of potentiality's emerging as actuality when conditions permit. Intention is such a condition. Eventually, even intention subsides as the will is surrendered to God.

CHAPTER 14

Enlightenment: The Presence of Self

Introduction

Positionalities result in the problematic dualities of the ego experienced as presumptions. These result in the ego's projections, which it erroneously believes to be reality. Collectively, they constitute the illusions of Descartes' *res interna* (*cogitans*), which means that they are the products of emotions and mentations. The purpose of spiritual work is the elimination of this primary barrier in order to discover *res externa/extensa* (essence) as Reality revealed as Creation, that is, the world as it is (essence) and not as it is perceived or appears to be. The transition from illusion (*res cogitans*) to Reality requires not a change of content but of context and, therefore, of paradigm. The Realization of Reality is the consequence of a shift to identification with experiential context instead of content and is, therefore, a major shift of paradigm.

The emergence of the Real is a spontaneous Effulgence that is consequent to removing the limitations of perception and its barriers. The transcendence of limitation is the result of intention and subordination of the personal will, with its illusory gains and payoffs, to Divine Will.

While the state or condition of what has been called Enlightenment is celebrated, its exact nature has only been alluded to by analogy, and it has also tended to become 'mythologized'. Thus, terms like 'the Supreme', 'the Ultimate, or 'the Absolute' tend to attract glamorization and fantasy elaborated by imagination. The state of Enlightenment is not a superimposition nor does it depend on the addition of a quality.

The subject is the condition. Similarly, the condition or state is not a 'claim', as there is no personal claimant. What is expressed verbally is simply a statement of facts that report the condition, which is merely a confirmation of the Reality of its Source once again. Thus, the condition is also not an achievement nor does it imply accomplishment. Nothing is gained by glamorization of the state, which is far beyond the possibility of exaggeration. Despite the effulgent nature of the condition, description serves the purpose of communication, which is essentially a revalidation of the Reality of Divinity.

Preceding Stages

The transition from the experiencer of the ego/self to the Presence of the Self is very major. Because of its prior experience, the mind has the expectation that such a state will really be an extension of itself or will be some kind of 'otherness' and therefore new and unfamiliar. Neither expectation is correct.

As the levels of consciousness are transcended, the quality of experiencing changes in ways that have already been described (*Transcending the Levels of Consciousness*). Both the world and the subjective self become progressively more benign, compassionate, and loving. In the high 500s, the flow of the kundalini energy has begun to transform observation and subjective experiencing to levels of inner joy, and the world appears ever more beautiful and incredible. The perfection of all things shines forth. This leads not only to joy but also eventually to an indescribable ecstasy that precludes worldly function. When even that wondrous state is surrendered to God, it is replaced by an all-pervasive stillness, silence, and peace that are even beyond ecstasy in its wonder.

Within the intrinsic beauty, the sacredness of all Creation emanates forth from within as well as beyond form. The formless Essence of Divinity radiates out via form itself. Progressively, the linear is replaced by a nonlinear Oneness. The Allness of Divinity is strongly confirmed by the immense power of Love as intrinsic to Creation and Divinity. The Presence of Love is all pervasive and experienced as one's intrinsic Self. It melts linearity into Oneness, which is simultaneously exquisitely gentle and, paradoxically, infinitely powerful.

As has already been described, if the devotee has been following the pathway of negation, what may emerge next is the high illusion of the Void as the Ultimate Reality. The pathway presents infinite Oneness and nonlinear perfection and is all inclusive, infinite, and beyond time or location. (This illusion occurs at calibration level 850, as mentioned previously.) The Void is to be recognized and refused if it is devoid of Love. From this point on, one proceeds not by negation but by affirmation, which is reinforced by deep prayer and supplication to God for guidance. (Divine Love is not to be confused with the emotionality/attachment of what is ordinarily perceived as human love.)

As the qualities and context of each stage are surrendered to God, a final confrontation arises that also has to be surrendered, and it is challengingly confrontive. The devotee needs to be adequately prepared because failure at what could be called the 'final door' may result in very severe dejection that may last for more than just one lifetime. The serious student needs to know well in advance, therefore, that at the very last doorway, they will be confronted with their willingness to surrender life itself, or at least to that which has been believed since the beginning of evolution to be the very core of life itself. This final gateway is very rarely passed, and one reason is the lack of preparation, lack of certainty, and a final doubt of major magnitude. Therefore, for the deeply committed, very serious student only, the following section is provided.

The Final Doorway

As this approaches, the entire context is pristine, pure, formless, and nonlinear. There are no 'others' nor is there anywhere to turn. There are no longer any personal qualities or positionalities, nor is thinkingness available, as the mind is silent and nonconceptual. There are no images or memories. Consciousness alone remains as awareness itself, with no object or content of that consciousness awareness. It merely *is* of its own, with neither subject nor object. It is awareness itself that is aware, and there is no remaining 'entity' that is aware.

At this point, awareness is identified with the quality of life itself. That is all that is left—just 'life'. This sense of the pure core of life has lost its prior qualifications, adjectives, verbs, or nouns. These have been surrendered long before. All that is left is just the pure quality of life itself as the core of existence. Then arises a progressive fear, which compounds to almost terror, that this, too, must be surrendered at the doorway. Thus arises the fear of absolute death or annihilation into nothingness and nonexistence forever. At this point, it is obvious that what is to be surrendered to God is the life of the self and its motive to continue to exist as the experiencer and seeming source and substrate of life (the last illusion). This is a very strong illusion and to face it takes courage, faith, conviction, and the very depth of devotion: "To Thee, O Lord, do I surrender life itself."

Because the mind is silent, it cannot be consulted. In its place arises a Knowingness that appears as a result of the vibrational frequency within the aura that has been absorbed from the Knowingness of an Enlightened Teacher somewhere in time. The Knowingness is that 'all fear is illusion'. This must be known with absolute certainty. Ignore the terror, for it is really what could be called 'the final test', and surrender life itself. That one is actually dying is confirmed because that is the inner experience. This is the one and only death that can ever occur, and it arises because it has never before been surrendered. Physical death is relatively nothing at all. There is a sudden leaving of the body, and life goes on, reemerging as another embodiment. Thus, this confrontation is the first and only time it will ever have to be faced and surrendered. As one lets go, there are a few moments of dread, and then the doorway opens to the Infinite Splendor and Glory that is beyond all description.

Revelation

The mind remains silent, and there is an immense awe as Creation now appears as Revelation—iridescent, radiant as though enchanted, and vibrant with the efflorescence of unmistakable Divinity. All is as though in intense Technicolor—electrified and luminous. All is conscious and conscious of being conscious, and conscious of the awareness of consciousness of all else that exists. All is intrinsically worshipful as a consequence of the conscious awareness of the Presence of God as Creation in its most minute details. All is Holy and Sacred, as evidenced by its splendor as Existence itself. Therefore, all things are seen as sacred and holy; all things 'both large and small' are sacred; thus, "*Gloria in Excelsis Deo!*"

Even texture itself is prominent and seems to be transformed into an aliveness with a radiant quality. All is alive and its intrinsic Essence shines forth as a presentation that is inclusive of recognition as an innate, worshipful quality. All is equal by virtue of its Essence, its perfection, and its efflorescent luminosity. The Glory of God is far beyond the capacity of comprehension, and instead, there is a contextual Self-identity that one *is* what is being comprehended, and yet there is nothing to really comprehend. At this point, description has to stop because of the duality of languaging. Transcending that final doorway required the surrender of the seeming core and source of life itself. There is the overwhelming astonishment at the discovery that all that exists *is* Creation as an expression of Divinity, and the field of consciousness pervades all that exists. Thus Divinity is intrinsic to all that exists, as well as to the awareness of that Reality. All that exists reflects the Divinity of its Source. Paradoxically, by surrendering life, one discovers Life.

Even the presence of the physical body is too

peripheral to be noticed. However, it is later rediscovered as sort of a surprise. It continues to function on its own, spontaneously and autonomously. There is no 'self' or primary or causal agency to determine or decide its actions. It operates autonomously as a consequence of its interaction with the field of context. Its continuance is not a matter of interest, and it just seems to 'know' what to do all by itself.

The transformational quality of the Oneness of Creation is the consequence of the disappearance of 'the experiencer'. There is no 1/10,000th-of-a-second delay that automatically edits all of experience as a consequence of the prior operations of the ego. Therefore, the transformed appearance of All and its interpretations have been removed, and one is now identical with the essence of the unfolding of Creation rather than its edited translation. One is no longer experiencing the 'tape monitor' of life but the very existential core of Life itself. The analogy is like the difference between hearing a full philharmonic orchestra in person and listening to a tape recording of its performance.

Adjustment

The transition is far more major than can be imagined, described, or even anticipated. However, the information provided allows for the successful transition through this very major final period. Initially, there is paradigm shock, sometimes referred to as 'God shock'. There is a profound awe of such a major dimension that the mind remains silenced forever. There no longer is a volitional personal self nor its presumed inner causal-agent quality, and the sense of 'I' now includes all of Existence, beyond time, dimension, or linear description. There is no longer any feeling of 'mine', nor any feeling of having qualities of possession or control. All is Self-existent and Self-fulfilling. The performance of the body is autonomous and a consequence of its relationship to the overall field. It is witnessed that the body, just as before, avoids getting run over by traffic, but it does it all by itself. Although there is no mentalization as such, information is still available because of the unique quality of the field of consciousness itself that impersonally records all events, no matter how seemingly trivial. The Knower and the Known are identical Realities as a consequence of consciousness/awareness. Dualistic thinkingness disappears as an operating system. In its place, it is stunningly obvious that meaning *is* Essence and the Reality of Essence *is* its meaning. Thus, as obvious or absurd as it might sound, a chair *is* its meaning.

The major transformation is followed by a period of reorientation to all the former qualities of life and senses of even the whereabouts of the body itself and its relationship to other objects. People address the body as 'you' and think that the 'you' is the body. The Self is silent, invisible and has no actual name as such.

The period of reorientation and readjustment may be quite lengthy and actually take years. During this time, there emerges an autonomous operational quality that one might call the persona/personality agent that is interactive with the world. Life continues on of its own because Existence is Life. Potentiality emerges as actuality as a consequence of evolution. From the above, it is apparent that there is no 'person' to become enlightened; on the contrary, the person disappears and is replaced by that nonlinear Reality. Therefore, it is obvious that the state is not an accomplishment, an achievement, an acquisition, nor even a transformation. It is actually a replacement.

Fulfillment: The Actualization of Potentiality

The student asks how realistic or practical is it to set the realization of the Self, or Enlightenment, as it has been called, as a goal, considering its rarity. Over history, it has indeed been extremely rare. However, because of the progression of the overall evolution of consciousness within the last century, the likelihood of a committed student's reaching Enlightenment has increased by more than one thousand percent. Each advancement in consciousness is already an enlightened state by comparison to that which preceded it. To move from below calibration level 200 to above 200 is already a primary and very major step. The next major transition is to move from the dominance of emotionality to the capacities of reason and the intellect, and then to transcend them at level 499 and realize that Reality is not linear or descriptive but instead subjective. The emergence of Love at 500 announces the dominance of a new paradigm. Consciousness level 540 signals the emergence of Unconditional Love, which progresses on through joy and ecstasy. Enlightenment classically calibrates at level 600 and then on up to 1,000 with the disappearance of linearity as the presumed reality.

Identification with limitation ceases, and the process then becomes one of transcending limiting contextualizations that are related to the emergence of the qualities or levels of consciousness by which the unmanifest becomes Manifest. Thus, the most advanced levels of consciousness have to do with expansion and dominion of nonlinear context and paradigms that are beyond precise linear description or definition.

Q: **The final blocks to Enlightenment itself sound rather formidable or at least difficult.**

A: They do so to the ego itself but not to the inner Truth and Knowingness of the Self. It is true that the final core of the ego is incapable of relinquishing its seeming sovereignty as the illusory source of life and existence. The strength is provided by the power of the Self that is at one with the Truth of Divinity. This knowingness is radiated as a consequence of Identity with the Absolute. Divinity is the Source of all Existence, including one's own. Fear arises from the ego/self which is dissolved into the Self. Thus, the very source of fear is eliminated and transcended.

The fear that is found at the end of the journey is unlike any fear that was faced previously. Its quality is existential and nonlinear rather than limited or discrete. Experientially, the fear was indeed very strong but not really stronger in intensity than prior fears that were overcome. What gave this fear a unique quality similar to dread was its identification as being equated with the source of existence and life itself.

The ego equates survival of life with control. In a final surrender of control, the underlying primordial fear arises. Life is a consequence of the Divinity of its Source, which is the ultimate confrontation to the very core of the ego.

Q: **Without instruction, the spiritual pathway would be more difficult, if not impossible. Enlightenment has been very rare.**

A: The consciousness level of humanity has been progressively rising, which collectively supports spiritual evolution and the availability of more advanced information about the qualities and nature of consciousness itself. Historical literature about very advanced states often described the states themselves but did not provide details of the incremental steps necessary to reach them.

Q: **The spiritual process itself seems like it must have been of lengthy duration.**

A: In this lifetime, the duration of the process was thirty-eight years. The onset itself was startling and dramatic at age three and has been described elsewhere. The presentation was a confrontation with voidness/nonexistence versus Allness as the Ultimate Reality. Thus, the way back to the Realization of Divinity as Infinite Love had to be rediscovered and transcended. The strong inflowing of kundalini energy, which is exquisite, gave confirmation that the pathway was provided by God. That had originally been experienced in this lifetime during early adolescence.

Q: **Was that a 'near-death' experience?**

A: No, it was not. Refuge was sought from icy winds in a remote area but the physical condition was strong and healthy. What was sought was merely the comfort of refuge. Then spontaneously occurred a subjective state that was transcendent, everlasting, primordial, and all encompassing. The Radiance of the Self as Infinite Love dissolved all fear of personal self or limitation. The duration was beyond time and even 'before all universes and after all universes have disappeared'. The Self replaced all limitations of personal self, including location, duration, or identification. Subsequently, all fear of death disappeared.

Q: It seems a strange paradox that years later you became an agnostic for some time.

A: That again was the consequence of an unanticipated revelation. It marked the end of belief in God as a belief system. It was subsequent to a sudden revelation of the total suffering of all mankind throughout all of human existence. It was a staggering confrontation.

Up until that time, religiosity had prevailed, but in shock and dismay at the revelation, the belief in a God who could allow or be the cause of all that suffering was unsustainable. At that time, the common prevailing belief was that God was the cause and creator of everything. What was being witnessed was the suffering that is the consequence of the ungodliness of the ego from which humanity needs a Savior.

Despite the collapse of religious belief in God, there persisted a drive to get to the core and source of Truth itself. That led to searching within during four years of deep classical clinical psychoanalysis, followed by three more years of depth analysis focused on uncovering the roots of the ego itself. The inner search then continued into reaching the very depths of the ego and the lower levels of Hell that, too, are experientially beyond the limitations of time. It was from the pits of eternal spiritual darkness that the call to God was answered for it took that extreme of agony and despair to crack the ego's tenacious hold. Subsequently, there was a period of oblivion, and then the shining forth of Divinity and the Glory of God was made Known and Revealed in all its stunning Beauty and Perfection. Creation shone forth as God Manifest *as* Creation.

Q: That was like a termination or end point to the unfoldment of the potential of Consciousness itself?

A: There had been prior advances as well as challenges. There was a very advanced state of consciousness that was accompanied by the Knowingness of now being beyond the limitations of personal karma. There emerged a nonlinear state best described as a condition consequent to a greatly expanded context of Reality. In the silence, unasked, there was heard and recognized a silent message that said, "Now that you are beyond all karmic answerability or accountability, even the limitations of personal love, all power is yours over others—own it—take it—use it, for there are no consequences."

Few in number had passed through these rarified gates, and it could be seen who had said yes to the temptation and who had refused power for its own sake and gain. I saw that Jesus had refused it and passed through, as had the great Avatars and Enlightened sages. While it is termed the 'Luciferic temptation', there was no entity present as a source

of the temptation. It was presented as a silent temptation: "All power over others is yours—claim it."

The temptation was refused by the Higher
Knowingness that the temptation was a false promise because the Ultimate Reality *is* the Source of all
Power. The Self *is* innately the Power and has no
need to claim it as an acquisition. Power for its own
sake as gain had no appeal. Frankly, it would have
been a burden. Subsequent to its refusal, the last
doorway opened up, and with the death of the ego,
the Glory of God shone forth and all went silent.

**Q: Thus temptations persist and reappear almost
to the end of the spiritual journey?**
A: That was the sequence. Subsequently, it was
recalled that Jesus Christ and the Buddha described
similar confrontive temptations.

Q: What of the physical systems?
A: Each major advance seemed to trigger a transitory
inner agony localized to the aura, or etheric body.
These were made more bearable by recalling that
both the Buddha and Jesus Christ had described
them. Jesus 'sweat blood' in the Garden of
Gethsemane; the Buddha was beset by attacks of
demons and felt as though his bones were broken.

This occurs from consciousness level 800 and
up and was recurrent at the passing of the high
gates. The reason is that from consciousness level
800 and up, negative regions from the collective
consciousness of mankind are being challenged
and transcended. One is aware that the positionalities being challenged are not those of personal

karma per se, that is, not that of the individual but the individual as reflective of the overall karmic inheritance of mankind itself.

Q: This kind of information is very rare indeed. Does an 'ordinary' seeker need to know it?

A: Yes, indeed, for today's beginner or mid-way seeker is tomorrow's enlightened sage. That others have crossed these barriers makes it easier for the next to break through them. This has been termed the 'Roger Bannister effect'. Each crossing leaves a vibrational track available for the next runner to 'know' that it *can* be done. Breaking through a major barrier requires an inner Knowingness that it is possible because it is based on the power and the invincible strength of Truth.

Those who seek Enlightenment deserve all the useful confirmed truth, knowledge, and encouragement that is available. Spiritual endeavor can result in major unexpected leaps without prior warning. It is the better part of wisdom to have such information beforehand.

CHAPTER 15

Progressive States of Consciousness

Introduction

Exposition thus far has been for the purpose of providing clarity to information that is somewhat difficult to put into language. The information, however, is comforting by providing some degree of familiarity through describing the subjective, evolutionary stages of consciousness that occur at the various levels. It is also reassuring to hear that seeming obstacles along the way are normal and not actually intrinsically personal as such but instead are consequent to the characteristics of a particular level of consciousness.

Evolutionary emergence of potential occurs as transitions that are rewarding and confirmatory overall. However, there are also transitory periods that are discomforting, and they are also to be expected. There may be periods of feeling estranged, depersonalized, or 'not like myself'. There may also be times of confusion or feeling 'spacey' or disorganized. These are due to the adjustments resulting from shifts of context and their experiential familiarity and customary sense of subjectivity. The sense of 'realness' or self-identity progressively expands and alters prior belief systems of 'who I am', as they transform into '*what* I am'. Therefore, there may be progressive changes in values, goals, and prioritization of time and effort. These transitional periods are temporary, and ease of transition is aided by prayer, spiritual practices, and especially, a contemplative lifestyle.

While the self may occasionally feel confused or discordant, the Self always knows exactly where 'you' are because the reality is always within the Province of

God. It is not possible to be lost, although on occasion a devotee may feel lost. The problem is not the condition itself but the fear of losing control and familiarity.

The infinite field of consciousness is all inclusive and in accord with all possible experiential ranges or states. The field is innately in harmonic balance and thereby inclusive of all transitional states. The overall field could be described as self-correcting, and consequently, it realigns itself in a compensatory manner. All alterations are time limited and temporary. Analogously, weather changes, but the atmospheric balance of the stratosphere is unaffected.

Subjectively, all that is needed to progress are patience, prayer, faith in the process, and the surrendering of resistances. Confusion, like the changes in the weather, is a transitional condition that clears with patience and also with emergence into the next stage, whereby the confusing condition is transcended. Divine harmony restores equilibrium in time. All is actually in Divine Order. It is not possible to get 'lost' to God anymore than a tennis ball gets lost to gravity just because it is temporarily bouncing.

Transitions or changes are consequent to the unfolding of evolution, which is the actualized expression of Creation. The process is both within and without, and every moment represents the emergence of the new. Life is lived on the advancing edge of the evolution of consciousness, and thus, all experiencing is evanescent and transitory.

Transcending the Attraction of Form
The evolution of consciousness may proceed in a variety of ways. It may be slow and sudden, or it may

proceed in an orderly fashion but then take sudden leaps. The major transitions occur when conceptual thought is abandoned along with interest in 'experiencing' or identification with the experiencer 'edge' of the ego/self and its processing functions. Beyond linear concepts and images, there is nothing that requires processing. Thus, the mind/self becomes silent, and instead, the nonlinear context prevails. It could be summarized as follows: Ego/mind *thinks*, field (consciousness) *knows*, and Self *is*.

It is really not difficult to become aware of the 'experiencer' aspect of the self that constantly processes input irrespective of the nature or qualities of the data, such as thoughts, memories, images, sensations, and emotions. With practice, one can stay focused on that quality of consciousness as a process without actually getting involved in the 'what' that is being processed or experienced. This experiential edge watchfully processes every second. It is like a listener/feeler/anticipator/rememberer/recognizer/multiprocessor unit. The 'experiencer' is the perceptual edge of consciousness awareness that is independent of the nature of the data being processed.

It is this quality that one identifies with as 'me' or 'I'. With observation, it will be recognized that this function is autonomous and impersonal, although the self claims it is identity. The experiencer is not a 'who' but an 'it'. It is an autonomous functionality. It is comparable to a multifunctional processing-probe faculty. The ego/self thrives on that 'experiencer' quality and is actually addicted to it.

By attention and volition, the seductive attraction of the experiencer can be refused. Succumbing to its entertainment is only a habit. It is not 'you' but only an activity with which the self becomes identified. The mind thinks that it will 'go blank' and become void without the constant linear input of information and focus on 'what is going on'. Yet, at night, sleep is a welcome relief from the experiencer's endless chatter. Thus, the mind thinks there are only three possibilities: (1) experiencing, (2) sleep (oblivion), or perhaps, (3) sleep with dreaming. But relatively unknown to ordinary mind is a fourth state, which is one of awareness itself and independent of content, experiencing, or even participating, analyzing, or recording. The underlying quality is effortless, peaceful, and compatible with a contemplative lifestyle. It leads to the states classically termed Samadhi.

Alignment with the Field of Consciousness/Awareness

With inner fixity of purpose, diligence, and discipline, the attraction of the data-processing experiencer function can be refused as a focus of interest, importance, or even identification. Beneath the emotionalized experiencer is the subtle silence of Awareness. Because it is devoid of the limitations of linear content or form, it is like a blank screen or the reflecting surface of a pool. It is the a priori condition without which there would be no knowingness of what the experiencer is experiencing, nor of what the witness/observer is perceiving.

This basic subtle state is a fundamental constant. It is akin to an overall space or field within which all other phenomena and conditions are encompassed. The silent, subtle field is a quality of the Self. This field, state, or condition of consciousness is all inclusive, yet devoid of identification with content. Awareness is aware of itself. As such, it is a fundamental, ever-existent quality.

This 'fourth state' of consciousness was described by Ramana Maharshi by its Sanskrit term, *turiya*. From this condition, all appears equal by virtue of the reality that meaning and existence are one and the same thing, that is, what things mean is fulfilled by what they *are*, and what they *are* is exactly the fulfillment of what they mean. Their existence is their meaning. (This awareness occurs at consciousness calibration level 750.)

This state is also discernible as the silent substrate out of which thoughts spontaneously emerge. It can be detected as the a priori condition which is the field or matrix that, in a split instant, precedes the emergence of thinkingness. Its 'location' is analogous to that of the ocean, just prior to the emergence of a flying fish. Each thought spontaneously arises and is not recognized until it has become fully formed. As it emerges, the thought is like a vague stirring of energy that quickly moves from indistinct form to more detailed and identifiable completion. The process is very rapid. To discern the silent field itself requires sharp attention and perspicacity. The technique is to refuse interest in the specificity of thoughts and stop trying to recognize or read them. Unless intended by volition, thoughts are just endless babble, and it is only the vanity of the ego that cherishes them as being entertaining or deserving of interest.

To bypass and transcend the seductive attraction of the content of stream-of-consciousness thinkingness, humility about its importance quickly reveals that without the projection of value, ninety-nine percent of thoughts are just plain boring and platitudinous. Disenchantment with them diminishes their attraction by withdrawal of interest. The other illusion is that attention to thoughts is necessary to survival, whereas in reality, survival is up to the Self. With sharp focus, it becomes apparent that thoughts can be relinquished earlier and earlier in the process of their emergence and formation. With continued focus and relinquishment of their entertainment value, they will slowly disappear as recognizable form and subside to just being a transitory urge to think. The gratification of this impulse can be refused. By doing this, it becomes amazingly apparent that one thinks only as a consequence of desiring to do so, and that thoughts and images only have an imaginary value. Intrinsically, they are not really stunningly marvelous. This discovery that one is really the source of thinkingness reveals that one is not the victim of the mind but the originator of the phenomenon by virtue of intention and desire. Freedom is a consequence of the deep humility which reveals that the only reason one thinks is because one wants to in order to derive an experiential benefit or payoff.

The ego/mind is afraid that if it doesn't think, it will (1) get bored, and (2) cease to exist. The problem of boredom is relatively easy to transcend simply by seeing that boredom is just the frustration of not being amused by 'interesting' thoughts. To transcend the thinkingness, interest should really be refocused on searching for the substrate out of which thinkingness arises. One can choose to be bored with thoughts, and upon examination, it will be clear that they are primarily just the constant reworking, over and over, of familiar concepts, images, and ideas.

The Self is quite capable of choosing and being in charge without the necessity of concepts. It is also easy to observe that the linearity of thinkingness merely leads to further linearity as a parade of ideas, images, memories, imaginings, and more. Curiosity can be shifted from the form and content of thoughts in order to become aware of the silent nascent field of consciousness awareness itself. Silence is of the Self; thoughts are of the self. The Self does not need encouragement by the investment of the energy of interest. The silent state can be intuited by both contemplation and meditation. One can merely assume the attitude of being too lazy to bother to think.

Spiritual Practice

The ego/mind is attracted to novelty and therefore searches frantically for interesting form and sensation. This can be refused and replaced by interest in the silent, formless substrate that is always present and merely has to be noticed. It is comparable to the silent background without which sound could not be discerned.

The phenomenal world is like a giant Rorschach card—the figure 'means' whatever one wishes it to. Sound is discernible only because it is superimposed against the background of silence, and thus form can only be recognized because it is superimposed within formless space. Likewise, the content of mind is only identifiable because of its formless, silent background screen. The experiencer can thus be directed to focus on the silent, formless backdrop. The substrate, because of its silence, has an innate feeling of peace. Silence and peace can be chosen, appreciated, valued, and welcomed as relief from the constant tension of the ever-watchful expectancy of the experiencer function. When peace is more valued than the entertainment of the insatiable ego, it will be discovered to be ever present and available. That one even has such an option is unknown by 99.7 percent of the population. Thus, there is an unknown freedom available: one can choose merely to refuse the ego investment in the world and one's thoughts about it (i.e., surrender it to God).

Renunciation

Traditionally, many serious spiritual devotees renounce the world and withdraw from it by retreat to environments that have low sensory input and do not require specific activity. For some students, that is very helpful and even necessary at different times, if even for only short periods, such as provided by formal retreats. As mentioned earlier, true renunciation is internal and is the consequence of a decision and an act of the will. On a practical level, actual physical withdrawal and renunciation are a declaration and a shift of social roles. Inner renunciation may also result in withdrawal from the world but not for the same reasons.

From the calibration levels of the high 500s on up, participation in the world is problematic. Major alterations of lifestyle may be mandatory as well as preferred. Rural simplicity and peacefulness, as well as environmental beauty, become more concordant with one's inner state. Some devotees in the high 500s manage to continue to teach or write. At the levels of the 600s and 700s, all participation may stop, and statistically, many who reach these levels choose the option to leave the body; however, some remain for the fulfillment of karmic propensities. In the high levels, function is the consequence of Divine Ordinance, as the personal will has been surrendered to God. 'Motivation', 'intention', or 'goals' no longer exist. Actions are autonomous, spontaneous, and consequent to the Presence as Self.

Awareness of the overall silent contextual field is facilitated by a contemplative lifestyle that could be likened to shifting interest from details to 'the big picture'. It 'gets' overall qualities of atmosphere without going into specifics and therefore intuits generalities rather than thinking or analyzing details. The resistance of the ego/mind is that it is afraid it might 'miss' something, as it is addicted to processing the details of the content of form, which is the attraction and lure of the world. To 'renounce the world' means to withdraw energy from it and decline activities that require attention to specifics, thereby abiding in the Self rather than in the amusements of the self.

As a result of the withdrawal from interest in the world, it may be abandoned. Many devotees cease following the news via newspapers or television. It is quickly discovered that it never was the world that was interesting but the projections by one's ego of its values and the specifics of its sensations. The brain is the sense organ of the experiencer, and one realizes that it is destined for physical death. Therefore, the importance of the Self rather than the self is realized by accepting the inevitability of mortality. It is only necessary to shift from devotion to the world to devotion to God and the Spirit.

One's life span is already determined at the very moment of birth (verified repeatedly by consciousness research). The devotee is thus one who surrenders one's life to God rather than to the ego/mind experiencer's projected values of the world.

While abandoning the world may sound drastic in the early stages of the spiritual quest, it occurs quite naturally and is welcomed with relief later on. At advanced stages, some functioning in the world may return but is of a different nature as there is no longer anything to 'get' from the world. It is primarily the scene of evolution/creation in which all is of equal value by virtue of its existence.

Q: **The emphasis has been on de-energizing the ego and its illusions. What about the identification of the self with the body?**

A: It is true that many traditional spiritual practices and teachings often start with and emphasize the body as well as attempts to control the energies of the chakra system. However, their meaning, importance, and value are the consequence of mental/emotional processes by the ego. It seems to be of greater pragmatic value to emphasize the deconstruction of the ego/self to begin with.

The body itself is actually not experienced; instead, only the *sensations* of the body are experienced. For example, one experiences the whereabouts, position, comfort, etc., of the arm but not the arm itself. This is easily verified if sensation is prevented by the cutting of a nerve. Therefore, awareness of the body is merely composite sensation by which the somatic sensory area of the brain records input, and by neuronal function, replicates the body image. The 'phantom limb' phenomenon that is sometimes seen clinically is a neurological anomaly whereby the brain produces, out of habit, a false image of a nonexistent limb that has been lost due to amputation. This is classified as a sensory hallucination.

During sleep, sensory input is discontinued and the body passes out of conscious subjective awareness. Thus, the experience of the body is conditional.

The attachment to the body is to sensation and the superimposition of the concept of 'mine'; and what is 'mine' and is controlled by 'me' must therefore be 'who I am'. Identification with the body is consequent to the ego's positionalities. To detach from identification of self as the body, it is necessary only to see the body as an 'it' rather than a 'me'. Even when characterized as 'me', it becomes obvious that one does not have real dominion over probably ninety-nine percent of its overall functions (biochemical, digestive, cardiovascular, neuronal, metabolic, etc.) Thus, even control of the body is only in its grossest functions.

Now imagine that a limb has been lost in an accident. The person still calls the body 'me'. This continues even if more physical attributes are lost—limbs, facial characteristics, or sensory loss (e.g., Helen Keller). Thus, the 'body' as 'me' is a mentalization. There is the fictional story of *Donovan's Brain* in which only his brain survives and is kept alive via artificial means. Relentlessly, the 'brain' kept right on with its ego positions, such as the desire to control others and survive. Helen Keller, on the other hand—deaf, mute, and blind—calibrated in the high 500s. Joseph Merrick, the "Elephant Man," so-called due to severe facial disfigurement, calibrated at the level of a high saint (590).

The sense of 'who' we are is primarily an identification with the body, the personality, and its mentalization, with accompanying emotional investment. One can do an internal mental imaging process to see how much of the body or its sensations could actually be lost and yet the self retain a sense of 'I'. It becomes clear that the experiential 'I' *has* a body but *is not* a body.

The classic approach to detachment from identification of self with the body is to detach from the sensory dependence on physicality for pleasure and gratification. These have to do with desire and the searching for pleasure as an external acquisition. Asceticism decreases the sovereignty of the illusion that the source of happiness, pleasure, and gratification is external, for even if its locus is external, the sense of pleasure and gratification is an internal function. The body is a functional utility mechanism, and pleasure is not the consequence of bodily function but the gratification of desire itself. Similar gratification can be obtained in a hypnotic state wherein the body itself is not given a reward but only the image is suggested. The body is therefore a mechanism and not a source.

With spiritual practice focused directly on the ego and its experiencer function, the importance and identification of self with the body automatically diminish of their own accord. When meaning, significance, and value are withdrawn from it, the body-image sense recedes and only recurs when actually necessary (e.g., to sleep, eliminate, hydrate, etc.) In the state of Bliss (cal. 600), or even at the consciousness levels of the higher 500s, the seeming needs of the body diminish. One can dance tirelessly for hours in ecstasy and go without food for days in Samadhi/Bliss. In higher states, care of the body may be neglected, as its importance is lost when no longer hypothesized to be the self.

Q: Detachment from the world is correlated with detachment from the body as well?

A: They go hand in hand in that their perception gives them value. When individuals have an out-of-body experience, the sense of 'me' floats up in space also. One then looks down at the body disinterestedly. It is perceived as almost foreign to one's sense of reality. Return to the body is done only reluctantly, or it happens spontaneously with a sudden jarring sensation. It is not really possible to identify with the body or value it when one is not 'in' it. People who have learned how to leave the body in trained altered states of consciousness often have to be trained in how to return to the body on a given command.

Q: Is 'out of body' anything similar to the 'near-death' experience?

A: They are quite dissimilar. Subjectively, the near-death experience is transformative due to the power of the presence of Divine Love. The person's calibrated level of consciousness is thereby advanced and characterized by the loss of the fear of death. Paradoxically, the out-of-body experience does not result in a change in consciousness level. This would imply that the awareness that the self is nonphysical is already known at a certain level but forgotten in ordinary life.

If we pose the question using consciousness research techniques, the answer that calibrates as true is that the knowledge that we are not a body but a spirit is already known but merely forgotten as a consequence of incarnation. Thus, the sense of self is independent of the body but associated with the sense of being a localized identity rather than a physicality.

It is entertaining to go "out of body" or even to travel considerable distances, but the experience does not appear to be of any significant long-term benefit to the advancement of the level of consciousness itself. It is a relatively frequent occurrence during surgery (well-known to surgeons) and also after severe accidents. Nurses and doctors have learned (often rather ruefully) that their conversations while the patient was supposedly asleep and presumably unconscious were 'heard' by the patient who later related them verbatim to the surprised staff.

Q: Consciousness research has revealed a great deal of helpful information. It clarifies understanding and recontextualizes the spiritual evolutionary process. It is also confirmation of spiritual reality and its progressive experiences. Do not the basic fundamentals, however, remain the same?

A: The essential fundamental principles for spiritual endeavor are still those that are time-honored, such as devotion, humility, fortitude, willingness to surrender, and faith and trust in God. These are reinforced by dedication, prayer, and the supplication and invocation of God's Grace by an act of the Spiritual Will. Although critical information about the ego and the levels of consciousness facilitates transformation, confirmation stems from the application of the fundamental spiritual principles described. These are empowered by intention, which results in alignment and integration whereby the basic principles become operative. Devotion is a consequence of assent by the will. Complete and total surrender to God can eclipse the process at any given point along the way.

Q: What statement would summarize a whole life of spiritual experience and dedication?

A: *Gloria in Excelsis Deo!*

Section Three

Appendices

APPENDIX A

CALIBRATION OF LEVELS OF TRUTH OF THE CHAPTERS

Explanatory Note

Languaging of material into printed form lowers the calibration level from its origin by fifteen points.

The Book *Discovery of the Presence of God* overall   955

APPENDIX B

MAP OF THE SCALE OF CONSCIOUSNESS

God-view	Self-view	Level	Log	Emotion	Process
Self	Is	Enlightenment	700-1,000	Ineffable	Pure Consciousness
All-being	Perfect	Peace	600	Bliss	Illumination
One	Complete	Joy	540	Serenity	Transfiguration
Loving	Benign	Love	500	Reverence	Revelation
Wise	Meaningful	Reason	400	Understanding	Abstraction
Merciful	Harmonious	Acceptance	350	Forgiveness	Transcendence
Inspiring	Hopeful	Willingness	310	Optimism	Intention
Enabling	Satisfactory	Neutrality	250	Trust	Release
Permitting	Feasible	Courage	200	Affirmation	Empowerment

▲

LEVELS OF TRUTH

LEVELS OF FALSEHOOD

▼

Indifferent	Demanding	Pride	175	Scorn	Inflation
Vengeful	Antagonistic	Anger	150	Hate	Aggression
Denying	Disappointing	Desire	125	Craving	Enslavement
Punitive	Frightening	Fear	100	Anxiety	Withdrawal
Uncaring	Tragic	Grief	75	Regret	Despondency
Condemning	Hopeless	Apathy, hatred	50	Despair	Abdication
Vindictive	Evil	Guilt	30	Blame	Destruction
Despising	Hateful	Shame	20	Humiliation	Elimination

APPENDIX C

HOW TO CALIBRATE THE LEVELS OF CONSCIOUSNESS

General Information

The energy field of consciousness is infinite in dimension. Specific levels correlate with human consciousness, and these have been calibrated from "1" to "1,000." (See Appendix B: Map of the Scale of Consciousness.) These energy fields reflect and dominate human consciousness.

Everything in the universe radiates a specific frequency or minute energy field that remains in the field of consciousness permanently. Thus, every person or being whoever lived and anything about them, including any event, thought, deed, feeling, or attitude, is recorded forever and can be retrieved at any time in the present or the future.

Technique

The kinesiological response (muscle testing) is a simple "yes" or "not yes" (no) response to a specific stimulus. It is usually done by the subject's holding out an extended arm and the tester pressing down on the wrist of the extended arm, using two fingers and light pressure. Usually the subject holds a substance to be tested over their solar plexus with the other hand. The tester says to the test subject, "Resist," and if the substance being tested is beneficial to the subject, the arm will be strong. If it is not beneficial or has an adverse effect, the arm will go weak. The response is very quick and brief.

It is important to note that the intention, as well as both the tester and the one being tested, must calibrate over 200 in order to obtain accurate responses.

The higher the levels of consciousness of the test team, the more accurate are the results. The best attitude is one of clinical detachment, posing a statement with the prefix statement, "In the name of the highest good, _____ calibrates as true. Over 100. Over 200," etc. The contextualization "in the highest good" increases accuracy because it transcends self-serving personal interest and motives.

For many years, the test was thought to be a local response of the body's acupuncture or immune system. Later research, however, has revealed that the response is not a local response to the body at all, but instead is a general response of consciousness itself to the energy of a substance or a statement. That which is true, beneficial, or pro-life gives a positive response that stems from the impersonal field of consciousness, which is present in everyone living. This positive response is indicated by the body's musculature going strong. For convenience, the deltoid muscle is usually the one best used as an indicator muscle; however, any of the muscles of the body can be used, such as the gastrocnemias, which are often used by practitioners such as chiropractors.

Before a question (in the form of a statement) is presented, it is necessary to qualify 'permission'; that is, state "I have permission to ask about what I am holding in mind." (Yes/No) Or, "This calibration serves the highest good."

If a statement is false or a substance is injurious, the muscles go weak quickly in response to the command "Resist." This indicates the stimulus is negative, untrue, anti-life, or the answer is "no." The response is fast and brief in duration. The body will then rapidly recover and return to normal muscle tension.

There are three ways of doing the testing. The one that is used in research and also most generally used requires two people: the tester and the test subject. A quiet setting is preferred, with no background music. The test subject closes their eyes. *The tester must phrase the 'question' to be asked in the form of a statement*. The statement can then be answered as "yes" or "not yes" (no) by the kinesiological response. For instance, the *incorrect* form would be to ask, "Is this a healthy horse?" rather than make the statement, "This horse is healthy," or its corollary, "This horse is sick."

After making the statement, the tester says "Resist" to the test subject who is holding the extended arm parallel to the ground. The tester presses down with two fingers on the wrist of the extended arm sharply, with mild force. The test subject's arm will either stay strong, indicating a "yes," or go weak, indicating a "not yes" (no). The response is short and immediate.

A second method is the "O-ring" method, which can be done alone. The thumb and middle finger of the same hand are held tightly in an "O" configuration, and the hooked forefinger of the opposite hand is used to try to pull them apart. There is a noticeable difference of the strength between a "yes" and a "no" response. (Rose, 2001).

The third method is the simplest, yet, like the others, requires some practice. Simply lift a heavy object, such as a large dictionary or merely a couple of bricks, from a table about waist high. Hold in mind an image or true statement to be calibrated and lift. Then, for contrast, hold in mind that which is known to be false. Note the ease of lifting when truth is held in mind and the greater effort necessary to lift the load when the issue is false (not true). The results can be verified using the other two methods.

Calibration of Specific Levels

The critical point between positive and negative, between true and false, or between that which is constructive or destructive, is at the calibrated level of 200 (see Map). Anything above 200, or true, makes the subject go strong; anything below 200, or false, allows the arm to go weak.

Anything past or present, including images or statements, historical events, or personages, can be tested. They need not be verbalized.

Numerical Calibration

Example: "Ramana Maharshi's teachings calibrate over 700." (Y/N)

Or, "Hitler calibrated over 200." (Y/N) "When he was in his 20s." (Y/N) "His 30s." (Y/N) "His 40s." (Y/N) "At the time of his death." (Y/N)

Applications

The kinesiological test cannot be used to foretell the future; otherwise, there are no limits as to what can be asked. Consciousness has no limits in time or space; however, permission may be denied. All current or historical events are available for questioning. The answers are impersonal and do not depend on the belief systems of either the tester or the test subject. For example, protoplasm recoils to noxious stimuli and flesh bleeds. Those are the qualities of these test materials and are impersonal. Consciousness actually knows only truth because only truth has actual existence. It does not respond to falsehood because falsehood does not have existence in Reality. It will also not respond accurately to nonintegrous or egoistic questions, such as should one buy a certain stock.

Accurately speaking, the kinesiological response is either an "on" response or it is merely "not on." Like the electrical switch, we say the electricity is "on," and when we use the term "off," we just mean that it is not there. In reality, there is no such thing as "off-ness." This is a subtle statement but crucial to the understanding of the nature of consciousness. Consciousness is capable of recognizing only Truth. It merely fails to respond to falsehood. Similarly, a mirror reflects an image only if there is an object to reflect. If no object is present to the mirror, there is no reflected image.

To Calibrate A Level

Calibrated levels are relative to a specific reference scale. To arrive at the same figures as in the chart in Appendix A, reference must be made to that table or by a statement such as, "On a scale of human consciousness from 1 to 1,000, where 600 indicates Enlightenment, this _____ calibrates over _____ (a number)." Or, "On a scale of consciousness where 200 is the level of Truth and 500 is the level of Love, this statement calibrates over _____." (State a specific number.)

General Information

People generally want to determine truth from falsehood. Therefore, the statement has to be made very specifically. Avoid using general terms such as a "good" job to apply for. "Good" in what way? Pay scale? Working conditions? Promotional opportunities? Fairness of the boss?

Expertise

Familiarity with the test brings progressive expertise. The "right" questions to ask begin to spring forth and can become almost uncannily accurate. If the same tester and test subject work together for a period of time, one or both of them will develop what can become an amazing accuracy and capability of pin-pointing just what specific questions to ask, even though the subject is totally unknown by either one. For instance, the tester has lost an object and begins by saying, "I left it in my office." (Answer: No.) "I left it in the car." (Answer: No.) All of a sudden, the test subject almost 'sees' the object and says, "Ask, 'On the back of the bathroom door.'" The test subject says, "The object is hanging on the back of the bathroom door." (Answer: Yes.) In this actual case, the test subject did not even know that the tester had stopped for gas and left the jacket in the restroom of a gasoline station.

Any information can be obtained about anything

anywhere in current or past time or space, depending on receiving prior permission. (Sometimes one gets a 'no', perhaps for karmic or other unknown reasons.) By cross-checking, accuracy can be easily confirmed. For anyone who learns the technique, more information is available instantaneously than can be held in all the computers and libraries of the world. The possibilities are therefore obviously unlimited, and the prospects breathtaking.

Limitations

Approximately ten percent of the population is not able to use the kinesiological testing technique for as yet unknown reasons. The test is accurate only if the test subjects themselves calibrate over 200 and the intention of the use of the test is integrous and also calibrates over 200. The requirement is one of detached objectivity and alignment with truth rather than subjective opinion. Thus, to try to 'prove a point' negates accuracy. Sometimes married couples, also for reasons as yet undiscovered, are unable to use each other as test subjects and may have to find a third person to be a test partner.

A suitable test subject is a person whose arm goes strong when a love object or person is held in mind, and it goes weak if that which is negative (fear, hate, guilt, etc.) is held in mind (e.g., Winston Churchill makes one go strong and bin Laden makes one go weak).

Occasionally, a suitable test subject gives paradoxical responses. This can usually be cleared by doing the "thymic thump," as was discovered by Dr. John

Diamond. (With a closed fist, thump three times over the upper breastbone, smile, and say "ha-ha-ha" with each thump and mentally picture someone or something that is loved.)

The imbalance may be the result of recently having been with negative people, listening to heavy metal rock music, watching violent television programs, playing violent video games, etc. Negative music energy has a deleterious effect on the energy system of the body for up to one-half hour after it is turned off. Television commercials or background are also a common source of negative energy.

As previously noted, the kinesiological method of discerning truth from falsehood and the calibrated levels of truth has strict requirements. Because of the limitations, calibrated levels are supplied for ready reference in prior books, and extensively in *Truth vs. Falsehood*.

Explanation

The kinesiological test is independent of personal opinion or beliefs and is an impersonal response of the field of consciousness, just as protoplasm is impersonal in its responses. This can be demonstrated by the observation that the test responses are the same whether verbalized or held silently in mind. Thus, the test subject is not influenced by the question, as they do not even know what it is. To demonstrate this, do the following exercise:

The tester holds in mind an image unknown to the test subject and states, "The image I am holding in mind is positive" (or "true," or "calibrates over 200," etc.). On direction, the test subject then resists the downward pressure on the wrist. If the tester holds a positive image in mind (e.g., Abraham Lincoln, Jesus, Mother Teresa, etc.), the test subject's arm muscle will go strong. If the tester holds a false statement or negative image in mind (e.g., bin Laden, Hitler, etc.), the arm will go weak. Inasmuch as the test subject does not know what the tester has in mind, the results are not influenced by personal beliefs.

Correct Kinesiological Technique

Just as Galileo's interest was in astronomy and not in making telescopes, the Institute for Advanced Spiritual Research is devoted to Consciousness research and not specifically to kinesiology. The DVD, *Power vs. Force* (Veritas Publishing, [1995], 2006), demonstrates the basic technique. More detailed information about kinesiology can be found on the Internet by searching for 'kinesiology'. Numerous references are provided, such as the College of Applied Kinesiology (www.icak.com), and other educational institutions.

Disqualification

Both skepticism (cal. 160) and cynicism calibrate below 200 because they reflect negative prejudgment. In contrast, true inquiry requires an open mind and honesty devoid of intellectual vanity. Negative studies of behavioral kinesiology *all* calibrate below 200 (usually at 160), as do the investigators themselves.

That even famous professors can and do calibrate below 200 may seem surprising to the average person.

Thus, negative studies are a consequence of negative bias. As an example, Francis Crick's research design that led to the discovery of the double helix pattern of DNA calibrated at 440. His last research design, which was intended to prove that consciousness was just a product of neuronal activity, calibrated at only 135.

The failure of investigators who themselves, or by faulty research design, calibrate below 200 (all calibrate at approximately 160), confirms the truth of the very methodology they claim to disprove. They 'should' get negative results, and so they do, which paradoxically proves the accuracy of the test to detect the difference between unbiased integrity and nonintegrity.

Any new discovery may upset the apple cart and be viewed as a threat to the status quo of prevailing belief systems. That a clinical science of consciousness has emerged that validates spiritual Reality is, of course, going to precipitate resistance, as it is actually a direct confrontation to the dominion of the narcissistic core of the ego itself, which is innately presumptuous and opinionated.

Below consciousness level 200, comprehension is limited by the dominance of Lower Mind, which is capable of recognizing facts but not yet able to grasp what is meant by the term 'truth' (it confuses *res interna* with *res externa*), and that truth has physiological accompaniments which are different from falsehood. Additionally, truth is intuited as evidenced by the use of voice analysis, the study of body language, papillary-response EEG changes in the brain, fluctuations in breathing and blood pressure, galvanic skin response, dowsing, and even the Huna technique of measuring the distance that the aura radiates from the body. Some people have a very simple technique that utilizes the standing body like a pendulum (fall forward with truth and backward with falsehood).

From a more advanced contextualization, the principles that prevail are that Truth cannot be disproved by falsehood any more than light can be disproved by darkness. The nonlinear is not subject to the limitations of the linear. Truth is of a different paradigm from logic and thus is not 'provable', as that which is provable calibrates only in the 400s. Consciousness research kinesiology operates at level 600, which is at the interface of the linear and the nonlinear dimensions.

Discrepancies

Differing calibrations may be obtained over time or by different investigators for a variety of reasons:

1. Situations, people, politics, policies, and attitudes change over time.
2. People tend to use different sensory modalities when they hold something in mind, i.e., visual, sensory, auditory, or feeling. "Your mother" could therefore be how she looked, felt, sounded, etc., or Henry Ford could be calibrated as a father, as an industrialist, for his impact on America, his anti-Semitism, etc.

One can specify context and stick to a prevailing modality. The same team using the same technique will get results that are internally consistent. Expertise develops with practice. There are some people, however, who are incapable of a scientific, detached attitude and unable to be objective, and for whom the kinesiological method will therefore not be accurate. Dedication and intention to the truth have to be given priority over personal opinions and trying to prove them as being "right."

APPENDIX D

REFERENCES

Adler, J., V. Juarez, et al. (and editorial staff). 2005. "Spirituality in America." Special Report. *Newsweek*, August-September, 46-66.

Anderson, S., and P. Ray. 2000. *The Cultural Creatives: How 50 Million People Are Changing the World*. New York: Harmony Books.

Armandariz, Y. 2005. "Dalai Lama's Message: Compassion for Others." *Arizona Republic*, 16 September. (Address to Garvin School of International Management on individual responsibility.)

Bailey, A. 1950. *Glamour: A World Problem*. New York: Lucis Press.

Benoit, H. [1955] 1990. *Zen and the Psychology of Transformation: The Supreme Doctrine*. Rochester, Vt.: Inner Traditions - Bear & Company.

Bletzer, J. G. 1986 *Donning International Encyclopedic Psychic Dictionary*. Virginia Beach, Va.: Donning Publishing Co.

Bristow, D., et al. 2005. "Blinking suppresses the neural response to unchanging retinal stimulation." University College London, Institute of Neurology, as published in *Current Biology* 15, 1296-1300, 26 July.

Crick, C., and C. Koch. 1992. "The Problem of Consciousness." *Scientific American*, 267, September, 152-159.

Descartes, R. 1952. In *Great Books of the Western World*, vol. 31. Chicago: Encyclopedia Britannica.

Diamond, J. 1979. *Behavioral Kinesiology*. New York: Harper & Rowe.

—. 1979. *Your Body Doesn't Lie*. New York: Warner Books.

Few, B. 2005. "What We Know and What We Don't Know about Consciousness Science." *Journal of Consciousness Studies* 12:7, July, 74-87.

Gladwell, M. 2002. *The Tipping Point: How Little Things Can Make a Big Difference*. Boston: Back Bay Books.

Godman, D., ed. 1985. *Be As You Are: The Teachings of Ramana Maharshi*. Boston: Arkana.

Goodheart, G. 1976. *Applied Kinesiology:* 12th ed. Detroit: Goodheart. (Out of print).

James, W. [1902] 1987. *The Varieties of Religious Experience: A Study in Human Nature*. Reprint. Cambridge, Mass.: Harvard University Press.

Jung, C. J. 1979. *Collected Works*. Princeton, N.J.: Princeton University Press.

Keller, H.. and R. Shattuck, Ed. 2004. *The World I Live in/Helen Keller*. New York: New York Review Books Classics.

Hayakawa, S. 1971. *Our Language and Our World; Selections from Etc.: A*

Review of General Semantics, 1953-1958. New York: Harper Collins.

Henderson, R. 2005. Sermon, May 1. Science of Mind Center, Prescott, Arizona.

Lamsa, G. 1957. *Holy Bible from Ancient Eastern Manuscripts*. Philadelphia: A. J. Holmes Co.

Lewis, J., Ed. 2001. *Odd Gods: New Religions and the Cult Controversy*. Amherst, NY: Prometheus Books.

Mackay, C. [1841] 2003. *Extraordinary Popular Delusions & the Madness of Crowds*. Hampshire, U. K.: Harriman House.

Maharaj, N. [1973] 1999. *I Am That: Talks with Sri Nisargadatta Maharaj*. (4th Rev. ed.) Bombay: Chetana Private, Ltd.

Maharshi, R. [1972] 2004. *The Spiritual Teaching of Ramana Maharshi*. Boulder, Col.: Shambhala

Maslow, A. 1971. *The Farther Reaches of Human Nature*. New York: Viking Press.

Monroe, R. 1992. *Journeys Out of the Body*. (Rev.) New York: Main Street Books.

Partridge, C., Ed. 2003. *UFO Religions*. London: Routledge. (Unarius, Aetherius Society, Heaven's Gate, Scientology, Unification Church, Family of God, etc.)

Po, Huang, 1958. *The Zen Teaching of Huang Po: On Transmission of Mind*. (J. Blofield, trans.) New York: Grove Press.

Powell, R. 1999. *Discovering the Realm Beyond Appearance: Pointers to the Inexpressible*. San Diego: Blue Dove Press.

Rose, G. 2001. *When You Reach the End of Your Rope...Let Go*. Los Angeles: Awareness Press. ("O-Ring" kinesiological test method.)

Ruell, D. 1989. *Chaotic Evolution and Strange Attractors: The Statistical Analysis of Time Series for Deterministic Nonlinear Systems*. New York: Cambridge University Press.

—. 1980. "Strange Attractors." *Mathematical Intelligence* 2, 126-137. (Nonlinear dynamics, attractor fields.)

Sadlier, S. 2000. *Looking for God: A Seeker's Guide to Religious and Spiritual Groups of the World*. New York: Berkeley Publishing Group, Penguin Putnam.

Simpson, L. 1999. *The Book of Chakra Healing*. New York: Sterling Publishing.

Suzuki, D. T. 1991. *The Zen Doctrine of No-Mind: The Significance of the Sutra of Hui-Neng*. Boston: Weiser Books.

Thompson, J., and H. B. Stewart. 2002. (2nd ed.) *Nonlinear Dynamics and Chaos*. . New York: John Wiley & Sons.

Tolson, J. 2005. "Divided We Stand." *US News & World Report,* 42-48. 8 August. (God and country.)

Walsh, M. 1991. *Butler's Lives of the Saints: Concise Edition, Revised and Updated*. San Francisco: HarperSanFrancisco.

Watts, A. [1957] 1999. *The Way of Zen*. New York: Vintage

—. [1955] 1972. *The Way of Liberation in Zen Buddhism*. Society for Comparative Philosophy, Alan Watts Journal; 2nd ed.

ABOUT THE AUTHOR

Biographical and Autobiographical Notes

Dr. Hawkins is an internationally known spiritual teacher, author, and speaker on the subject of advanced spiritual states, consciousness research, and the Realization of the Presence of God as Self.

His published works, as well as recorded lectures, have been widely recognized as unique in that a very advanced state of spiritual awareness occurred in an individual with a scientific and clinical background who was later able to verbalize and explain the unusual phenomenon in a manner that is clear and comprehensible.

The transition from the normal ego-state of mind to its elimination by the Presence is described in the trilogy *Power vs. Force* (1995) which won praise even from Mother Teresa, *The Eye of the I* (2001), and *I: Reality and Subjectivity* (2003), which have been translated into the major languages of the world. *Truth vs. Falsehood: How to Tell the Difference* (2005) and *Transcending the Levels of Consciousness* (2006) continue the exploration of the ego's expressions and inherent limitations and how to transcend them.

The trilogy was preceded by research on the Nature of Consciousness and published as the doctoral dissertation, *Qualitative and Quantitative Analysis and Calibration of the Levels of Human Consciousness* (1995), which correlated the seemingly disparate domains of science and spirituality. This was accomplished by the major discovery of a technique that, for the first time in human history, demonstrated a means to discern truth from falsehood.

The importance of the initial work was given recognition by its very favorable and extensive review in *Brain/Mind Bulletin* and at later presentations such as the International Conference on Science and Consciousness. Many presentations were given to a variety of organizations, spiritual conferences, church groups, nuns, and monks, both nationally and in foreign countries, including the Oxford Forum. In the Far East, Dr. Hawkins is a recognized "Teacher of the Way to Enlightenment" (Tae Ryoung Sun Kak Dosa).

In response to his observation that much spiritual truth has been misunderstood over the ages due to lack of explanation, Dr. Hawkins presented monthly seminars that provided detailed explanations which are too lengthy to describe in book format. Recordings are available, along with questions and answers that provide additional clarification.

The overall design of this lifetime work is to recontextualize the human experience in terms of the evolution of consciousness and to integrate a comprehension of both mind and spirit as expressions of the innate Divinity that is the substrate and ongoing source of life and Existence. This dedication is signified by the statement "Gloria in Excelsis Deo!" with which his published works begin and end.

Biographic Summary

Dr. Hawkins has practiced psychiatry since 1952 and is a life member of the American Psychiatric Association and numerous other professional organizations. His national television appearance schedule has included *The McNeil/Leher News Hour, The Barbara Walters Show, The Today Show*, science documentaries, and many others.

He is the author of numerous scientific and spiritual publications, books, videotapes, and lecture series. Nobelist Linus Pauling coauthored his landmark book, *Orthomolecular Psychiatry*. Dr. Hawkins's diverse background as researcher and teacher is noted in his biographical listings in *Who's Who in America* and *Who's Who in the World*. He was a consultant for many years to Episcopal and Catholic Dioceses, The Monastery, monastic orders, and the Zen Monastery.

Dr. Hawkins has lectured widely, with appearances at Westminster Abbey; the Universities of Argentina, Notre Dame, and Michigan; Fordham and Harvard Universities; and the Oxford Forum. He gave the annual Landsberg Lecture at the University of California Medical School at San Francisco. He is also a consultant to foreign governments on international diplomacy and was instrumental in resolving long-standing conflicts that were major threats to world peace.

In recognition of his contributions to humanity, in 1995 Dr. Hawkins became a knight of the Sovereign Order of the Hospitaliers of St. John of Jerusalem, which was founded in 1077.

Autobiographic Note

While the truths reported in this book were scientifically derived and objectively organized, like all truths, they were first experienced personally. A lifelong sequence of intense states of awareness beginning at a young age first inspired and then gave direction to the process of subjective realization that has finally taken form in this series of books.

At age three, there occurred a sudden full consciousness of existence, a nonverbal but complete understanding of the meaning of "I Am," followed immediately by the frightening realization that "I" might not have come into existence at all. This was an instant awakening from oblivion into a conscious awareness, and in that moment, the personal self was born and the duality of "Is" and "Is Not" entered my subjective awareness.

Throughout childhood and early adolescence, the paradox of existence and the question of the reality of the self remained a repeated concern. The personal self would sometimes begin slipping back into a greater impersonal Self, and the initial fear of non-existence, the fundamental fear of nothingness, would recur.

In 1939, as a paperboy with a seventeen-mile bicycle route in rural Wisconsin, on a dark winter's night I was caught miles from home in a twenty-below-zero blizzard. The bicycle fell over on the ice and the fierce wind ripped the newspapers out of the handlebar basket, blowing them across the ice-covered, snowy field. There were tears of frustration and exhaustion and my clothes were frozen stiff. To get out of the wind, I broke through the icy crust of a high snow bank, dug out a space, and crawled into it. Soon the shivering stopped and there was a delicious warmth, and then a state of peace beyond all description. This was accompanied by a suffusion of light and a presence of infinite love that had no beginning and no end and was undifferentiated from my own essence. The physical body and surroundings faded as my awareness was fused with this all-present, illuminated state. The mind grew silent; all thought stopped. An infinite Presence was all that was or could be, beyond all time or description.

After that timelessness, there was suddenly an awareness of someone shaking my knee; then my father's anxious face appeared. There was great reluctance to return to the body and all that that entailed, but because of my father's love and anguish, the Spirit nurtured and reactivated the body. There was compassion for his fear of death, although, at the same time, the concept of death seemed absurd.

This subjective experience was not discussed with anyone since there was no context available from which to describe it. It was not common to hear of spiritual experiences other than those reported in the lives of the saints. But after this experience, the accepted reality of the world began to seem only provisional; traditional religious teachings lost significance and, paradoxically, I became an agnostic. Compared to the light of Divinity that had illuminated all existence, the god of traditional religion shone dully indeed; thus spirituality replaced religion.

During World War II, hazardous duty on a minesweeper often brought close brushes with death but there was no fear of it. It was as though death had lost its authenticity. After the war, fascinated by the complexities of the mind and wanting to study psychiatry, I worked my way through medical school. My training psychoanalyst, a professor at Columbia

University, was also an agnostic; we both took a dim view of religion. The analysis went well, as did my career, and success followed.

I did not, however, settle quietly into professional life. I fell ill with a progressive, fatal illness that did not respond to any treatments available. By age thirty-eight, I was *in extremis* and knew I was about to die. I didn't care about the body but my spirit was in a state of extreme anguish and despair. As the final moment approached, the thought flashed through my mind, "What if there is a God?" So I called out in prayer, "If there is a God, I ask him to help me now." I surrendered to whatever God there might be and went into oblivion. When I awoke, a transformation of such enormity had taken place that I was struck dumb with awe.

The person I had been no longer existed. There was no personal self or ego, only an Infinite Presence of such unlimited power that it was all that was. This Presence had replaced what had been "me," and the body and its actions were controlled solely by the Infinite Will of the Presence. The world was illuminated by the clarity of an Infinite Oneness that expressed itself as all things revealed in their infinite beauty and perfection.

As life went on, this stillness persisted. There was no personal will; the physical body went about its business under the direction of the infinitely powerful but exquisitely gentle Will of the Presence. In that state, there was no need to think about anything. All truth was self-evident and no conceptualization was necessary or even possible. At the same time, the physical nervous system felt extremely overtaxed, as though it were carrying far more energy than its circuits had been designed for.

It was not possible to function effectively in the world. All ordinary motivations had disappeared along with all fear and anxiety. There was nothing to seek, as all was perfect. Fame, success, and money were meaningless. Friends urged the pragmatic return to clinical practice, but there was no ordinary motivation to do so.

There was now the ability to perceive the reality that underlay personalities: the origin of emotional sickness lay in people's belief that they *were* their personalities. And so, as though of its own, a clinical practice resumed and eventually became huge.

People came from all over the United States. The practice had two thousand outpatients, which required more than fifty therapists and other employees, a suite of twenty-five offices, and research and electroencephalic laboratories. There were a thousand new patients a year. In addition, there were appearances on radio and network television shows, as previously mentioned. In 1973 the clinical research was documented in a traditional format in the book, *Orthomolecular Psychiatry*. This work was ten years ahead of its time and created something of a stir.

The overall condition of the nervous system improved slowly, and then another phenomenon commenced. There was a sweet, delicious band of energy continuously flowing up the spine and into the brain where it created an intense sensation of continuous pleasure. Everything in life happened by synchronicity, evolving in perfect harmony; the miraculous was commonplace. The origin of what the world would call miracles was the Presence, not the personal self. What remained of the personal "me" was only a witness to these phenomena. The greater "I," deeper than my former self or thoughts, determined all that happened.

The states that were present had been reported by others throughout history and led to the investigation of spiritual teachings, including those of the Buddha, enlightened sages, Huang Po, and more recent teachers such as Ramana Maharshi and Nisargadatta Maharaj. It was thus confirmed that these experiences were not unique. The *Bhagavad-Gita* now made complete sense. At times the same spiritual ecstasy reported by Sri Ramakrishna and the Christian saints occurred.

Everything and everyone in the world was luminous and exquisitely beautiful. All living beings became Radiant and expressed this Radiance in stillness and splendor. It was apparent that all mankind is actually motivated by inner love but has simply become unaware; most lives are lived as though by sleepers unawakened to the awareness of who they really are. People around me looked as though they were asleep and were incredibly beautiful. It was like being in love with everyone.

It was necessary to stop the habitual practice of meditating for an hour in the morning and then again before dinner because it would intensify the bliss to such an extent that it was not possible to function. An experience similar to the one that had occurred in the snow bank as a boy would recur, and it became increasingly difficult to leave that state and return to the world. The incredible beauty of all things shone forth in all their perfection, and where the world saw ugliness, there was only timeless beauty. This spiritual love suffused all perception and all boundaries between here and there, then and now, or separation disappeared.

During the years spent in inner silence, the strength of the Presence grew. Life was no longer personal; a personal will no longer existed. The personal "I" had become an instrument of the Infinite Presence and went about and did as it was willed. People felt an extraordinary peace in the aura of that Presence. Seekers sought answers but as there was no longer any such individual as David, they were actually finessing answers from their own Self, which was not different from mine. From each person the same Self shone forth from their eyes.

The miraculous happened, beyond ordinary comprehension. Many chronic maladies from which the body had suffered for years disappeared; eyesight spontaneously normalized and there was no longer a need for the lifetime bifocals.

Occasionally, an exquisitely blissful energy, an Infinite Love, would suddenly begin to radiate from the heart toward the scene of some calamity. Once, while driving on a highway, this exquisite energy began to beam out of the chest. As the car rounded a bend, there was an auto accident; the wheels of the overturned car were still spinning. The energy passed with great intensity into the occupants of the car and then stopped of its own accord. Another time, while I was walking on the streets of a strange city, the energy started to flow down the block ahead and arrived at the scene of an incipient gang fight. The combatants fell back and began to laugh, and again, the energy stopped.

Profound changes of perception came without warning in improbable circumstances. While dining alone at Rothman's on Long Island, the Presence suddenly intensified until every thing and every person, which had appeared as separate in ordinary perception, melted into a timeless universality and oneness. In the motionless Silence, it became obvious that there are no "events" or "things" and that nothing actually "happens" because past, present, and future are merely artifacts of perception, as is the illusion of a separate "I" being subject to birth and death. As the limited, false self dissolved into the universal Self of its true origin, there was an ineffable sense of having returned home to a state of absolute peace and relief from all suffering. It is only the illusion of individuality that is the origin of all suffering. When one realizes that one *is* the universe, complete and at one with All That Is, forever without end, then no further suffering is possible.

Patients came from every country in the world, and some were the most hopeless of the hopeless. Grotesque, writhing, wrapped in wet sheets for transport from far-away hospitals they came, hoping for treatment for advanced psychoses and grave, incurable mental disorders. Some were catatonic; many had been mute for years. But in each patient, beneath the crippled appearance, was the shining essence of love and beauty, perhaps so obscured to ordinary vision that he or she had become totally unloved in this world.

One day a mute catatonic was brought into the hospital in a straitjacket. She had a severe neurological disorder and was unable to stand. Squirming on the floor, she went into spasms and her eyes rolled back in her head. Her hair was matted; she had torn all her clothes and uttered guttural sounds. Her family was fairly wealthy; as a result, over the years she had been seen by innumerable physicians and famous specialists from all over the world. Every treatment had been tried on her and she had been given up as hopeless by the medical profession.

A short, nonverbal question arose: "What do you want done with her, God?" Then came the realization that she just needed to be loved, that was all. Her inner self shone through her eyes and the Self connected with that loving essence. In that second, she was healed by her own recognition of who she really was; what happened to her mind or body didn't matter to her any longer.

This, in essence, occurred with countless patients. Some recovered in the eyes of the world and some did not, but whether a clinical recovery ensued did not matter any longer to the patients. Their inner agony was over. As they felt loved and at peace within, their pain stopped. This phenomenon can only be explained by saying that the Compassion of the Presence recontextualized each patient's reality so that he or she experienced healing on a level that transcended the world and its appearances. The inner peace of the Self encompassed us beyond time and identity.

It was clear that all pain and suffering arises solely from the ego and not from God. This truth was silently communicated to the minds of the patients. This was the mental block in another mute catatonic who had not spoken in many years. The Self said to him through mind, "You're blaming God for what your ego has done to you." He jumped off the floor and began to speak, much to the shock of the nurse who witnessed the incident.

The work became increasingly taxing and eventually overwhelming. Patients were backed up, waiting for beds to open although the hospital had built an extra ward to house them. There was an enormous frustration in that the human suffering could be countered in only one patient at a time. It was like bailing out the sea. It seemed that there must be some other way to address the causes of the common malaise, the endless stream of spiritual distress and human suffering.

This led to the study of kinesiology, which revealed an amazing discovery. It was the 'wormhole' between two universes—the physical world and the world of the mind and spirit, an interface between dimensions. In a world full of sleepers lost from their source, here was a tool to recover and demonstrate for all to see— that lost connection with the higher reality. This led to the testing of every substance, thought, and concept that could be brought to mind. The endeavor was aided by my students and research assistants. Then a major discovery was made: whereas all subjects went weak from negative stimuli, such as fluorescent lights, pesticides, and artificial sweeteners, students of spiritual disciplines who had advanced their levels of awareness did not go weak as did ordinary people. Something important and decisive had shifted in their consciousness. It apparently occurred as they realized they were not at the mercy of the world but rather affected only by what their minds believed. Perhaps the very process of progress toward enlightenment could be shown to increase man's ability to resist the vicissitudes of existence, including illness.

The Self had the capacity to change things in the world by merely envisioning them; Love changed the world each time it replaced non-love. The entire scheme of civilization could be profoundly altered by focusing this power of love at a very specific point. Whenever this happened, history bifurcated down new roads.

It now appeared that these crucial insights could not only be communicated with the world but visibly and irrefutably demonstrated. It seemed that the great tragedy of human life had always been that the psyche is so easily deceived; discord and strife have been the inevitable consequence of mankind's inability to distinguish the false from the true. But here was an answer to this fundamental dilemma, a way to recontextualize the nature of consciousness itself and make explicable that which otherwise could only be inferred.

It was time to leave life in New York, with its city apartment and home on Long Island, for something more important. It was necessary to perfect myself as an instrument. This necessitated leaving that world and everything in it, replacing it with a reclusive life in a small town where the next seven years were spent in meditation and study.

Overpowering states of bliss returned unsought and eventually there was the need to learn how to be in the Divine Presence and still function in the world. The mind had lost track of what was happening in the world at large. In order to do research and writing, it was necessary to stop all spiritual practice and focus on the world of form. Reading the newspaper and watching television helped to catch up on the story of who was who, the major events, and the nature of the current social dialogue.

Exceptional subjective experiences of truth, which are the province of the mystic who affects all mankind by sending forth spiritual energy into the collective consciousness, are not understandable by the majority of mankind and are therefore of limited meaning except to other spiritual seekers. This led to an effort to be ordinary, because just being ordinary in itself is an expression of Divinity; the truth of one's real self can be discovered through the pathway of everyday life. To live with care and kindness is all that is necessary. The rest reveals itself in due time. The commonplace and God are not distinct.

And so, after a long circular journey of the spirit, there was a return to the most important work, which was to try to bring the Presence at least a little closer to the grasp of as many fellow beings as possible.

The Presence is silent and conveys a state of peace that is the space in which and by which all is and has its existence and experience. It is infinitely gentle and yet like a rock. With it, all fear disappears. Spiritual joy occurs on a quiet level of inexplicable ecstasy. Because the experience of time stops, there is no apprehension or regret, no pain, no anticipation; the source of joy is unending and ever present. With no beginning or ending, there is no loss or grief or desire. Nothing needs to be done; everything is already perfect and complete.

When time stops, all problems disappear; they are merely artifacts of a point of perception. As the Presence prevails, there is no further identification with the body or mind. When the mind grows silent, the thought "I Am" also disappears and Pure Awareness shines forth to illuminate what one is, was, and always will be, beyond all worlds and all universes, beyond time, and therefore without beginning or end.

People wonder, "How does one reach this state of awareness," but few follow the steps because they are so simple. First, the desire to reach that state was intense. Then began the discipline to act with constant and universal forgiveness and gentleness, without exception. One has to be compassionate towards everything, including one's own self and thoughts. Next came a willingness to hold desires in abeyance and surrender personal will at every moment. As each thought, feeling, desire, or deed was surrendered to God, the mind became progressively silent. At first, it released whole stories and paragraphs, then ideas and concepts. As one lets go of wanting to own these thoughts, they no longer reach such elaboration and begin to fragment while only half formed. Finally, it was possible to turn over the energy behind thought itself before it even became thought.

The task of constant and unrelenting fixity of focus, allowing not even a moment of distraction from meditation, continued while doing ordinary activities. At first, this seemed very difficult, but as time went on, it became habitual, automatic, requiring less and less effort, and finally it was effortless. The process is like a rocket leaving the earth. At first, it requires enormous power, then less and less as it leaves the earth's gravitational field, and finally, it moves through space under its own momentum.

Suddenly, without warning, a shift in awareness occurred and the Presence was there, unmistakable and all encompassing. There were a few moments of apprehension as the self died, and then the absoluteness of the Presence inspired a flash of awe. This breakthrough was spectacular, more intense than anything before. It has no counterpart in ordinary experience. The profound shock was cushioned by the love that is with the Presence. Without the support and protection of that love, one would be annihilated.

There followed a moment of terror as the ego clung to its existence, fearing it would become nothingness. Instead, as it died, it was replaced by the Self as Everythingness, the All in which everything is known and obvious in its perfect expression of its own essence. With nonlocality came the awareness that one is all that ever was or can be. One is total and complete, beyond all identities, beyond all gender, beyond even humanness itself. One need never again fear suffering and death.

What happens to the body from this point is immaterial. At certain levels of spiritual awareness, ailments of the body heal or spontaneously disappear. But in the absolute state, such considerations are irrelevant. The body will run its predicted course and then return from whence it came. It is a matter of no importance; one is unaffected. The body appears as an "it" rather than as a "me" as another object, like the furniture in a room. It may seem comical that people still address the body as though it were the individual "you," but there is no way to explain this state of awareness to the unaware. It is best to just go on about one's business and allow Providence to handle the social adjustment. However, as one reaches bliss, it is very difficult to conceal that state of intense ecstasy. The world may be dazzled and people may come from far and wide to be in the accompanying aura. Spiritual seekers and the spiritually curious may be attracted, as may be the very ill who are seeking miracles; one may become a magnet and a source of joy to them. Commonly, there is a desire at this point to share this state with others and to use it for the benefit of all.

The ecstasy that accompanies this condition is not absolutely stable; there are also moments of great agony. The most intense occur when the state fluctuates and suddenly ceases for no apparent reason. These times bring on periods of intense despair and a fear that one has been forsaken by the Presence. These falls make the path arduous and to surmount these reversals requires great will. It finally becomes obvious that one must transcend this level or constantly suffer excruciating "descents from grace." The glory of ecstasy, then, has to be relinquished as one enters upon the arduous task of transcending duality until one is beyond all oppositions and their conflicting pulls. But while it is one thing to happily give up the iron chains of ego, it is quite another to abandon the golden chains of ecstatic joy. It feels as though one is giving up God, and a new level of fear arises, never before anticipated. This is the final terror of absolute aloneness.

To the ego, the fear of nonexistence was formidable, and it drew back from it repeatedly as it seemed to approach. The purpose of the agonies and the dark nights of the soul then became apparent. They are so intolerable that their exquisite pain spurs one on to the extreme effort required to surmount them. When vacillation between heaven and hell becomes unendurable, the desire for existence itself has to be surrendered. Only once this is done may one finally move beyond the duality of Allness versus nothingness, beyond existence or nonexistence. This culmination of the inner work is the most difficult phase, the ultimate watershed, where one is starkly aware that the illusion of existence one here transcends is irrevocable. There is no returning from this step, and this specter of irreversibility makes this last barrier appear to be the most formidable choice of all.

But, in fact, in this final apocalypse of the self, the dissolution of the sole remaining duality of existence and nonexistence–identity itself–dissolves in Universal Divinity, and no individual consciousness is left to choose. The last step, then, is taken by God.

–David R. Hawkins

For a list of available audio and video recordings
and other publications on consciousness
and spirituality by Dr. Hawkins,
please contact:

Veritas Publishing
P. O. Box 3516
West Sedona, AZ 86340 U. S. A.
Phone: 928.282.8722   Fax: 928.282.4789
www.veritaspub.com